P9-DDC-826

IF I KNEW THEN...

IF I KNEW THEN...

AMY FISHER
AND ROBBIE WOLIVER

iUniverse, Inc.
New York Lincoln Shanghai

B FISHER
Fisher, Amy, 1974-
   If I knew then...

All Rights Reserved © 2004 by
Amy Fisher and Robbie Woliver

No part of this book may be reproduced or transmitted in any form
or by any means, graphic, electronic, or mechanical, including pho-
tocopying, recording, taping, or by an information storage retrieval
system, without the permission in writing from the publisher.

Published by iUniverse, Inc.

For information address:
iUniverse, Inc.
2021 Pine Lake Road, Suite 100
Lincoln, NE 68512
www.iuniverse.com

ISBN: 0-595-32445-2

Printed in the United States of America

Dedication

I dedicate this book to:

My mother, Rose, who visited me faithfully in Albion Correctional Facility, which is a ten-hour drive from Long Island. She never gave up on me, she constantly supported me through the mess I made of my life, and now she is there to share the good times.

My husband, Louis and my son, Brett, who have given me the perfect life. Through their love, courage, and support I developed the strength to reflect upon my mistakes, my pain, and the pain I caused.

Through this book, I hope I can help others through their own tough times.

I also dedicate this book to Marie La Pinta, who taught me there is hope, and not to give up because my life was only beginning. How right she was. This is a column I wrote about her for the *Long Island Press* in December 2002.

A TIME FOR CLEMENCY

About a month ago, I curled up on my favorite recliner with a hot cup of coffee and the Sunday paper. My 6 a.m. ritual—reading the paper quietly before my noisy family wakes up—is a relaxing way to ease into my day. (Well, relaxing as long as there are no articles about Amy Fisher!)

This particular Sunday, as I flipped through the paper, I came across an article called "Seeking Mercy for Mom." As I started reading, an overwhelming sadness came over me. It was about an elderly woman, Marie La Pinta, trapped in prison for 19 years over a domestic squabble that led to the death of her husband, Michael La Pinta.

A Suffolk County jury convicted La Pinta and her brother, Leonardo Crociata, on February 9, 1984, for a murder that their relatives say was the culmination of decades of physical and emotional abuse. Both are serving a 25-year-to-life prison sentence, although Marie was only charged as an accessory.

As I read the article, I felt helpless, wishing I could do something to help Marie gain her freedom. I believe strongly that society will be better served if she is released from prison. I say this not because I read some article, but because I know her.

I met Marie La Pinta in Bedford Hills prison in 1993. I was assigned to a horticulture program where I would sit by myself and draw pictures in the dirt to pass the time. I felt very isolated, and was not able to relate to the gangs, drugs, and violence that seemed to be the sociological norm of prison. There wasn't an abundance of young girls from the 'burbs to talk to.

In horticulture class, a kind, grandmotherly woman would ask me if I was all right. She would show me beautiful floral arrangements and offer to teach me how to create them. If I said, "No," she would simply smile and say, "Perhaps tomorrow." I had assumed she was one of the horticulture teachers, not realizing for a while that she, too, was a prisoner. She was so "normal" it never dawned on me that she could have been convicted of a crime. This was Marie, and indeed she had been convicted of a very serious crime.

I gravitated toward Marie's kindness, enjoying our afternoons together planting bulbs and making wreaths. It wasn't that I really liked the horticulture thing. I simply liked being around Marie. She was the only person I met there who was genuinely kind to me. Most people I came in contact with were too caught up in my notoriety to realize I was just a scared young kid from Long Island. Marie was different. Her biggest concern was that I was too skinny. Every afternoon she would bring me a home-cooked Italian meal. It was like having a close relative right there with me, so that I wasn't so alone.

I never asked Marie why she was in prison, assuming she was there for something trivial and would be going home soon. I figured that since she didn't ask me a bunch of nosy questions, I shouldn't be nosy either. She didn't speak much about herself; she was focused on helping other people.

Eventually, through prison gossip, I found out Marie was serving a 25-year prison sentence for the murder of her husband. I never asked Marie a single question about the situation leading to her arrest. I didn't have to—I knew there had to be extenuating circumstances.

Whenever I would feel sorry for myself, feeling as though my life was hopeless, I would think of Marie. She never complained and she was never bitter. I admired the way she lived her daily life, being productive and giving in spite of her dire circumstances.

When I was released from prison after seven years, I felt like I was being given a second chance at life. I vowed to show society that people make mistakes, but can learn from them and lead positive lives.

In 1999, I spoke to Marie's son, Tony, a Suffolk County attorney, asking him if there was anything I could do to help his mother. At the time, it probably would have become a joke— "Ha-ha, Long Island Lolita trying to free the convicts"—or something equally tabloidish.

We must forgive in order to move on. There are many circumstances surrounding Marie's conviction that call out for leniency. She was never accused of committing the murder itself, but she would not testify against her brother, the shooter, so she got the same sentence he did.

Marie's family is trying to secure clemency for her, as is the family of her deceased husband. Even tough-on-crime [former] District Attorney James Catterson, for the first time in his career, has recommended clemency.

Should Marie be given the opportunity to be a positive member of society? Does it really serve a purpose for her to be locked up in a prison after 20 years?

It is easy to say Marie's ordeal does not affect our daily lives, and therefore, it's not our problem. After all, she is not a friend or relative. It's easy to say, "Oh, how tragic," as we throw this newspaper in the trash. In the end, Marie's struggle is not our problem, right? But issues of fairness, redemption, and rehabilitation are part of the essence of what makes a society work.

Marie was an abused woman who was caught up in a situation out of her control. She has more than paid her dues. It is time to set her free.

For more information log on to www.MercyforMom.com.

For two years since this column ran, Marie has been denied clemency despite a wave of support from her family, the victim's family, the former DA, and ordinary citizens. This past year was the most frustrating because she went through extra legal stages that usually indicate the granting of clemency.

Contents

Acknowledgements:

From Amy: Thank you to Bruce Barket, my attorney, who fought endlessly for my freedom; and to Jed Morey for giving me a second chance at the *Long Island Press.*

From Amy and Robbie: Thank you to Susan Driscoll and iUniverse, Andree Abecassis and the Ann Elmo Agency, Jon Sasala, Michael Lesser, Sally Peterson, Cynthia Buck, Keith Hopkin and Sheri Woliver; and at the *Long Island Press*: Ron Morey, John Caracciolo, Bill Jensen, Michael Patrick Nelson, Edith Updike, Christopher Twarowski, Annie Blachley, Tim Bolger, Beverly Fortune, Gina DeGregorio, Kenny Herzog, Lauren E. Hill, Lauren Wolfe, Dave Gil de Rubio, Brendan Manley, Michael Conforti, Sandy O'Donnell, Mike Cali, Dave Patrick, Marie Piscatella, Tara Traina, Danny Chozahinoff, and Felice Cantatore.

From Robbie: Thank you to Amy, for letting me share your story; to Jed Morey, for your generosity and inspiration; to Bill Jensen, for your talent and support; to Bruce Barket, for the introduction to Amy; and especially to Marilyn Lash, Cory, Emma, and Shirley Woliver.

Art Direction: Jon Sasala
Cover Photo: Gary Zindel Photography; Laura Geller Make-Up Studio, NYC

Introduction

By Robbie Woliver

When the Amy Fisher scandal broke in 1992, I, like millions of others around the world, was glued to the story: a teenage girl shoots the wife of her lover in upper-class suburbia.

I was a true-crime buff, a Long Islander, and a journalist. And part of the story was taking place in my backyard. Literally. My next-door neighbor, Toby, it turned out, was the school nurse who sent Amy home from school that fateful day, and the media barrage Toby had to endure was quite stunning. I particularly liked the big bouquet from Geraldo, sent via limo.

As the scandal progressed and turned from a personal tragedy into a national obsession, some clear thinkers began changing the perspective on the story: Amy was the second victim. The story had been so overblown by the burgeoning tabloid '90s, an era fueled in part by this incident, that people lost sight of the fact that Amy was only sixteen when it began, and under the influence of an older man.

Let's just cut straight to the chase. If this archetypal girl-gone-bad tabloid story had occurred years later—today, for example—the media would have given far more scrutiny to Joey, the adult who influenced Amy so negatively, and written a different story.

The public's interest in and eventual compassion for Amy, disgust for Joey, and initial sympathy for Mary Jo were clouded by how big and cartoonish this story had become. Besides being the number-one story around the world, it inspired an unprecedented three movies. It also inspired a book I began working on at that time, *Sensational Long Island*, about the wild, notorious cases that have spewed from this interesting island.

In the late '90s, I worked at the *Long Island Voice*, the sister paper of the *Village Voice*, where I advocated getting the still-imprisoned but somewhat vindicated Amy Fisher to write a column for the paper. (Joey had, by this time, been convicted of Statutory Rape.) We heard that she had been taking writing courses, and word had it that she was into fashion. We thought she might be interested in a freelance job as our fashion columnist. But it was impossible to get through to her. It was during a particularly sensitive time in Amy's incarceration, and the efforts of her family and lawyer were concentrated on that. So we dropped the idea.

Soon after, I received a press release about some serious accusations Amy was making against the Albion Correctional Facility, the upstate New York prison in which she was incarcerated. I followed up, researched the story, interviewed Amy's mother, Rose—who, despite what anyone thought of Amy, was viewed with great compassion for her tireless work in defense of her daughter—and I concluded that Amy was being victimized in prison and that the story was now way beyond that of an out-of-control teenager shooting her lover's wife.

Eventually Amy was released on parole, thanks to the efforts of a new superstar lawyer, Bruce Barket, and a forgiving Mary Jo Buttafuoco. Amy was determined to make something positive out of her life. *What an opportunity she has*, I thought.

In 2000 the *Long Island Press* began publication as the *New Island Ear*. We were debuting with the story "Who We Are," and for research we conducted numerous Internet searches for "famous Long Islanders." Oh, there was the usual Billy Joel, Mariah Carey, Teddy Roosevelt, Walt Whitman, Jerry Seinfeld, and Billy Crystal—but number one, each time, was Amy Fisher. Yes, before Teddy Roosevelt!

As editor in chief of the start-up paper, I hired Bill Jensen, a friend, talented journalist, and fellow true-crime fanatic from my *Voice* days, to be managing editor. One of the first things we discussed in creating this new paper was getting Amy Fisher to write a column.

Within seconds of moving into our new digs, Bill was working his first assignment: calling Barket. It seemed like every hour I would annoy Bill with the suggestion "Call him back anyway." We finally got Bruce away from his more pressing business and made an offer, which he promised he would pass on to Amy.

Much to our surprise, Bruce called us back and told us that Amy had expressed interest. In retrospect, I am amazed, now that I personally see the daily barrage of requests she receives from the worldwide media and the letters sent to her by well-wishers. But as we later learned, the idea of a column, writing for a hometown paper and getting her story out, made sense to her.

Bill and I arranged to meet Amy and Bruce for dinner. We were informed that Amy had changed her name and undergone plastic surgery to change her appearance. When Bruce and Amy showed up, we were surprised to be greeted by a pretty young woman who looked more like a professional attending a business meeting than the young teen we recalled in cut-off jeans and flowing, eggplant-colored hair. But after all, she *was* attending a business meeting, and as I was soon to be reminded many times, this was a different person from the wild sixteen-year-old frozen in our memories.

Dinner was a first-class meal served in a beautiful, elegant private room in a restaurant owned by our paper's parent company. Okay, several people we knew dropped by under the pretense of seeing how things were going but really in the hope of catching a glimpse of the "Long Island Lolita." In fact, after the dinner one very hard-boiled journalist said to me, "Even if this doesn't work out, at least you can say you had dinner with Amy Fisher." Now having known her for several years, I see how almost everyone, no matter who they are, no matter how jaded they are, wants to "know" Amy Fisher.

Although Bill and I had been chasing Amy for years, her continued "celebrity" ten years after the crime was a surprise to us. We thought hers was a good story from a journalistic standpoint, and we felt like Long Islanders would have great interest in it. We had no idea that hiring Amy would attract the international attention it did—and that people still viewed her as some sort of media superstar.

People's reactions would soon make us realize how deeply Amy's story resonated. When she came to the *Press* office for the first time, a line of objective and very cynical reporters and editors would line up outside my office to borrow a pencil, pay back a dollar, return an e-mail from me in person, all under the guise of seeing Amy Fisher.

The dinner that first night went well. Conversation flowed easily, although Amy seemed a bit guarded. We offered her the job of writing a column, a fashion column, thinking that was what would reel her in. But she suggested something better.

We knew she had returned to college and completed a degree; at dinner Amy informed us that she had excelled in and enjoyed her writing classes. And while she was interested in fashion designing (and still is), she was not interested in writing about it. Why don't we begin with something more substantial, she suggested.

The conversation soon got serious, and it became obvious that she had a story to tell about her life since entering prison. Why not write an exclusive story about her life since her imprisonment? We'll see how that goes, she said, and if it works, we'll talk about a general column.

However huge the ultimate payoff for the paper, I knew that my workload as her editor had probably doubled, that I'd most surely have more than the usual editing work with this novice. But I knew we had hit the jackpot with her addition. What an amazing way to introduce our new publication, with this exclusive story that every media outlet in the world was trying to get.

Amy handed in her 3,000-word story, "Piecing My Life Back Together." On deadline. When I first read it, I couldn't believe how compelling it was. The story was extremely moving, incredibly insightful, funny, and, most surprisingly, extremely well written. I knew our readers would be very moved by learning who the real Amy Fisher was. (The entire story is reprinted in this book.)

As she recounted in her story, despite the fact that she was a good worker, once her employers found out who she really was (she had changed her name as well as her looks), their fear of the paparazzi would cause them to fire her. She was unable to hold on to a job. We thought, why not offer her one?

Our forward-thinking young publisher, Jed Morey, was incredibly enthusiastic and supportive. He appreciates themes of rehabilitation and redemption, and he liked the idea of giving this woman a second chance in life.

When her debut story broke, the worldwide publicity was overwhelming. We received a million hits to our website and hundreds of thousands of phone calls and e-mails. Every single publication and media outlet, it seemed, from *Newsweek* to Jay Leno to *The New York Times*, expressed interest in her. One CNN producer told me, when I asked about all the interest, "You're the hottest publication in the country. She is not one of those fifteen-minutes-of-fame celebrities [a sentiment later echoed by *The New York Times*]. Everyone is as interested in her today as they were when the story first broke. Plus everyone loves a happy ending."

Since then, Amy has written over seventy-five columns and features for us, ranging in theme from child-rearing (she's now a mom), dating older men, and advice to Lizzie Grubman and Martha Stewart to more serious topics like guns and kids, trouble signs in teens, prison issues, abortion, and news events like the Iraqi prison abuse scandal. Her beat is now mostly current events, true crime, and celebrity interviews for lifestyle features. And since Amy receives a lot of mail from people asking her for advice and very little of it can be answered personally, for a while she was answering readers' questions in her column.

During the years I've known her, Amy has let her guard down, and I have discovered a very serious, deep-thinking woman who lives with great remorse and guilt for what she did during her youth. She is also a fun-loving mom who spends much of her time in SpongeBob's world. I have very spirited conversations with her about politics and social issues, and I have great respect for her as a professional writer.

I watch her at her beautiful home, with her devoted husband and delightful young son, and I think about the turns in her life and what brought her to this positive point. I often catch her with a faraway look in her eye, and I can't imagine the dark days she must still have.

For a while, as her editor, I became her de facto spokesperson because she was adamant about holding on to her privacy. Although at times—when I was juggling calls from *Oprah* and *Dateline*, *People* and *US*, CNN and Fox, the *New York Post* and *USA Today*, feeling like Billy Flynn from *Chicago*—I questioned my new job description.

Why the book then, and why at this time? Every day I get proof that many people are interested in finding out more about Amy and where life has taken her. For Amy, the book is a way to finally set the record straight so that she can move on with her life. After telling what is finally a positive story, she doesn't want to dwell on her past again. She wants to move on to living her life and using her experience to help others.

Amy Fisher is still growing. It wasn't until she began writing this book that she came to the realization that she herself might also have been a victim, a theory that many people have held over the years. As unbelievable as this may seem, during the course of writing this book Amy called me with several startling and surprising revelations that had, for years, been on the minds of many other people.

Amy has lived with her guilt for so long and has spent so much time saying, "I'm sorry," that she has never really had time to reflect and heal. And despite books and articles attributed to her, she has never before been able to tell her own story in her own words, without any kind of demands or restrictions.

Amy has blossomed into an impressive columnist. She has great ideas, writes well, does good research, has strong natural journalistic instincts, and — what a joy this is to an editor — always delivers copy on or before deadline. She has become one of the most dependable writers on my staff.

The amount of attention she gets is almost incomprehensible. The large quantity of mail she receives ranges from those who say they are longtime supporters to people who were skeptics and are now devoted fans of her column. People pour their hearts out to her, telling heartbreaking stories of their own. Some ask if she has a fan club. Some start off by saying, "I was six when your story broke," or, "I'm in high school and I'm working on a report about you"; others write, "I'm a grandmother, and I'm so pleased to hear your life has gotten back on track," or, "I identify because I'm your age."

An extraordinary number of these letters tell Amy she is an "inspiration." Then there are the thousands of marriage proposals, autograph requests, job offers, "you're frickin' hot" e-mails, and "you go, girl" letters. They come from all across America, Canada, England, Japan, Australia. And Amy, to this day, doesn't understand why people are so attracted to, and ultimately moved by, her story.

The *Long Island Press* is a well-regarded publication, with many award-winning columnists. Amy's column is our most popular. But here's the telling part: At the beginning of her tenure at the *Press*, all of the mail she received was very personal — letters of support, questions about her life, and personal problems that readers wanted her to solve. Nowadays the great bulk of her mail is from readers responding to her smartly written columns on a wide variety of social, political, and moral issues — pure journalistic discourse.

As a person, Amy is complex. She is still chipping away at the wall she built around herself in prison. She has become a lot more complicated than she was when the world was introduced to her in 1992. No longer the "notorious girlfriend," she's now a mother, a wife, a journalist, an artist, and a woman with a conscience.

Amy has a new mission. As she has analyzed herself and her youth, she has become determined to set the record straight. She spent most of her life letting other people speak for her and not defending herself against outrageous accusations; she has come to a point in her life where she is now comfortable enough to tell her story. Hounded by the sensational media interest her case helped create, Amy has attempted to keep her life as private as possible. But there is still an insatiable public interest in her.

Every time she writes a story that has some broad interest, it is picked up by the wire services; every time a celebrity, like Martha Stewart, is on trial, she braces for the calls from the cable networks and national magazines for comment; whenever there's a turning point in her life, like getting married, the paparazzi are still outside her window. Ironically, the media outlets that have been the cruelest to Amy are the very media outlets that now grovel the most to get her to appear on their programs or write for their publications.

There are those countless *E! True Hollywood Stories*, *Biography*s, and *Headliners and Legends* that continuously air. Even *Saturday Night Live* recently made a cheap, outdated, and not very funny joke at her expense, as if that sixteen-year-old still exists. And then there are those three Made-For-TV movies about her. But more and more often when something about her is brought to public attention, a new, contemporary audience that is more sensitive to abuse, statutory rape, sexual predators, and pedophilia sees her story in a different and more objective light, free of the tabloid sensationalism that first generated her story.

Yes, there have been some positive changes in how the media views and treats Amy. Now publications and newspapers quote from her *Press* column. Now TV anchors report on something she wrote or something she's achieved as straight news, no longer snickering. Now more and more serious and credible publications and media outlets want to hear from her—although no matter how positive her message is, she is still referred to as the "Long Island Lolita," albeit with the modifier "former": "former Long Island Lolita speaks out on gun control"; "the former Long Island Lolita raises money for indigent prisoners." You know what? As long as the message gets through.

Her identity has been co-opted in many ways. It wasn't until recently that Amy finally won her fight against a company that had bought the domain www.amyfisher.com and was running it as a porn site. Thanks to attorney Michael C. Lesser, this past February she finally won the right to that domain, her own name.

Amy has never told her full story before. With this book, she is finally telling it—how and why it all happened—with the clarity that comes with the passage of time and with self-analysis. She talks about her youth, her family, her responsibility, Joey's role, and her perpetual remorse for Mary Jo. Outside of the courtroom, she has never before discussed her brutal time in prison, and she discusses her years there in painful detail. Her story about piecing her life back together after prison is moving and life affirming. She talks about her child and husband for the first time as well. She reflects on turning thirty. There are many never-before-published personal photos included. So candid is this book that Amy is even revealing her new appearance for the first time.

We've included some of Amy's columns from the *Long Island Press*. (All of her columns are archived on the *Press'* website, www.longislandpress.com.) A lot of reflection and personal philosophy are also included in this book. You can find suggestions from Amy on how a parent can take steps to prevent what happened to her from happening to their child and advice to teens on how to stay out of trouble. If Amy's story doesn't scare any troubled teen straight, perhaps nothing will.

Amy also provides information on organizations that help protect kids from getting involved with gun violence and some that work toward ending abuse in women's prisons—subjects on which she is, unfortunately, an expert. Proceeds from this book are being donated to several of those organizations.

So here is Amy Fisher's story—a story about a child who was stupid, reckless, manipulated, and frightened, told with the insight of someone who has experienced what few people have. In sharing with you how she turned her life around, it is Amy Fisher's hope that her story may motivate you in some way to change your own life or someone else's life for the better.

If tabloid shows didn't exist back in 1992, I would have just been on the regular news. People would have viewed me as the victim of this sexual predator.

I recently wrote a column about a young girl who ran off with her softball coach. She was around the age I was when I got involved with Joey. The FBI was looking for them. Would any law enforcement agencies have been looking for Joey Buttafuoco and Amy Fisher twelve years ago? Ha ha ha. No, twelve years ago it was all about putting the story on the front page of the *Enquirer*. Now there's more awareness about adults who prey on kids. Today they're not saying, "Oh well, she's old enough to understand what she's doing, let's ignore it." Nowadays they actually try to protect the teenager who's being victimized and help her when she's in trouble.

Amy Fisher
2004

Chapter One

JUDGING AMY

I thought about writing a book for a while. At first I wanted to write one that would give advice to parents on how to spot trouble signs in their kids and advice to kids on how to stay away from the kind of trouble I got into. After all, how many people can speak from the experience I had? What better poster girl to keep kids away from guns and out of trouble?

But I have received so much mail from people who want to know about my own life—what got me involved in this trouble in the first place, what the trouble was, what my time in prison was like, and how my life has been since prison—that I decided to do a little bit of both. Tell my story and, through my story, provide a life lesson or two.

The reality is that I don't care much to rehash my life. But I need to get it out there so I can get the facts straight and address the fictions that have been swirling around me for over a decade—and most importantly, move on.

So why get back into the public eye after years of much-appreciated privacy? My life is good. I have everything I need, although the things that are most important to me now are not really financial. What's most important is my family—I have a great extended family, a wonderful mom, a terrific husband, an amazing child, and another baby on the way.

For the last twelve years, every time I saw myself on television, I got butterflies in my stomach. I'm forever "the Long Island Lolita," and I don't want to be the Long Island Lolita. I want the things I've accomplished *since* I became that notorious teenager to be known. I'm tired of hiding. When I hear someone utter the words "Amy Fisher" in public—in a store or deli—for any reason, even if they don't know I'm standing there, it makes me sick in the pit of my stomach, and I want to run away and hide. Trust me, that's a bad feeling.

But my life has changed so much, and I am a much different person than I was when I first came into the public's consciousness, and although I committed a horrific act when I was a kid, I should also be judged as the woman I am today.

I'm thirty now. Turning thirty is a big life change for anyone, but for me it was bigger than for most, because I have been frozen in time to many people as a sixteen-year-old girl.

When I was sixteen years old, thirty seemed like a lifetime away. I thought it would take forever to get that old. Now that I have just reached that milestone, I don't feel old. In fact, I feel young. (I also lost seven years of my youth in prison.)

I'm now starting to believe I understand a little about life. I'm able to take a step back, and for the first time I'm able to really come to terms with my past choices and mistakes. I'm able to accept the harsh reality that I did certain things because I was selfish and lacked compassion for others. Today I'm able to admit this to myself. For the first time I am truly able to see that my mistakes were mine alone. Yes, there were negative influences that came my way, but I should have walked away, told my mom, asked for help. Throughout our lives we are all subject to negative influences; it is our responsibility not to fall prey to them.

I want people to see that I've turned my life around and that I'm a good person. It's important to me. I don't want to live my life always having to hide my Amy Fisher identity. Because even though I have a new name, a new appearance, and a new life, it still bothers me. I want people to accept me for who I am and who I've become, and I want them to see my accomplishments.

But I don't want to completely lose my past. I want to turn that terrible act that happened when I was a teenager into something that can help other kids who might be at risk.

The first thing I did upon being released from prison in 1999 was to change my name. I spent seven years being tortured by the media. I decided the only way to get rid of the Long Island Lolita moniker was to say good-bye to Amy Fisher.

I changed my name as well as my social security number. Everything was sealed through the courts and became inaccessible to the public. As you will read later, I also changed my physical appearance. I turned down many lucrative offers from the media, opting for a more private existence.

Staying off television and out of the public eye for the past five years has gradually given me the privacy I yearned for. I finally had what I thought I wanted, only to slowly realize it wasn't enough. I still had to deal with the Long Island Lolita legacy. I was the topic of the Biography Channel's *Lives of Crime*, A&E's *Biography*, *E! True Hollywood Story*, and *Headliners and Legends*, and through endless reruns I am constantly reminded of my past, as is the viewing public. My name and image are stuck in that time twelve years ago when the tabloids went crazy with my story, my image, and the facts. These shows just rehash distorted aspects of the tale, and only recently have they begun updating the successful and happy end of the story.

Whenever Joey Buttafuoco made a B-rated movie, appeared on Howard Stern's radio show, duked it out with a woman on *Celebrity Boxing*, or got arrested and wound up back in jail, the Long Island Lolita—and my sixteen-year-old face—suddenly made news again.

There seemed to be no escape.

I decided to face my fears; I decided to face myself, Amy Fisher.

I didn't wake up one day and say, "I want to turn my life around." I just grew through the stages of life from being a teenager to a young adult to where I am now. We all go through life progressions, and somehow, no matter who we are or what we've done, we mature and realize we want different things in life.

It wasn't a thunderbolt of an idea to say, "Okay, I'm going to be a writer and get married and have children." You hope for good things in your life, you work toward them, but you can't take them as a given. Especially when you screw things up as badly as I did.

But soon things start falling into place, and then it's all about how you live your life. After what I went through—and put other people through—I realized the importance of thinking about other people, having a positive outlook, and treating people well. And when you do that, people treat you well and the whole cycle begins again in a positive manner.

People always ask me if I changed as a person, if I became a more caring person. More caring than when I was a teenager? Absolutely. I think it's the rare, special teen who lives outside his or her own ego. While there are exceptions, most teenagers are spoiled and self-centered. They can be nice, bubbly, outgoing kids, but usually it's all about "*me.*"

It's "*my* clothes" and "*my* phone" and "take *me* here" and "*I* want a car" and "what else can you do for *me*?" and very rarely do they see anything outside of their immediate world. In that respect, I was a typical teen. But as you get older you start to realize that there are people around you and you start to develop compassion. Remarkably, even with everything I went through, it wasn't until my father passed away in 2000 that I began to think about life and death. I started questioning my own mortality, and it made me realize … I actually once thought about shooting somebody, and my God, I could have killed somebody, and that really meant that they would not be on this Earth anymore. As crazy as it sounds, when I committed the act, I wasn't thinking, *This person will not be on this Earth anymore.* All I thought was, *This is no big deal*, and I never insightfully thought about anything from beginning to end.

I didn't think about repercussions. That's how come I got in so much trouble. I never thought about what it meant to hurt a person in that way. I never thought that the end result would mean going to prison. I never even knew what a prison was really like. I was just so out of touch with reality. To me, prison was like the old *Charlie's Angels* episode when the three Angels are on a chain gang. I was just a kid who didn't know anything. If kids were aware of the repercussions of shooting someone...well, I wasn't one of those kids.

I didn't wake up one day and say, "I wanna shoot somebody today." It was Joey Buttafuoco, a then-thirty-five-year-old idiot, who put it into my head and told the naive teenage fool that I was that there would be no repercussions if I shot Mary Jo. He kept putting it into my head every day and glorifying criminal activity, glorifying things that were negative. And he got me to do a lot of terrible things, which I did because I was under his spell.

When I was young—I was fifteen when I first met Joey, who is eighteen years older than me—I knew adults who would buy us kids beer and cigarettes. (I have *never* had a beer, and I didn't smoke a cigarette until I was twenty-two.) So even though I didn't like beer, to me it was cool because the older people were cool, fun, and "with it," and they were encouraging us to partake. And then there was my mother, who was always saying, "Don't drink, don't smoke, do your schoolwork"—well, she was no fun. She was just a boring wet blanket to me. But when you're a mixed-up kid with no self-esteem, like I was, and you're encouraged to act recklessly by an adult who says he loves you, you think it's okay. An adult who glorifies negative behavior and takes a disturbed child under his wing is a recipe for disaster. And then, before you know it, you become an adult and look back at it and realize what a fool you were and how horrible the situation really was.

There isn't a day that goes by that I don't think about what I did. I think about Mary Jo and wish her peace and the best life can offer her. And now that she is divorced from Joey, her life has to be improved. I think about their kids and wish them peace and happiness as well. As a mother now myself, I can't imagine what they went through.

Chapter Two

BAD INFLUENCE

While I was let down by a number of adults, I was under the influence of only one—Joey Buttafuoco. He was the child who never grew up. His whole life revolved around criminality. I just don't know how he gets away with the things he does, committing one despicable act after the next.

Joey was very into being a mobster wannabe, insinuating he was in the Mafia, and when you're sixteen years old you're thinking, *Oooh, the Mafia. That's kind of cool.* And it's even worse today than when I was a child. My generation didn't even have *The Sopranos*. Nowadays kids are bombarded with glorified violent images on TV, in movies, in video games, and even in their music.

From my experience, the most obvious piece of advice I can offer parents is to control the graphic, criminal, and often violent images your kids see. Cut TV time; supervise movies, videos, and music. You might find my conservative stance a bit ironic, but think about it. Who would know better than me?

I was a nice upper-class suburban girl who was seduced by these images, and look where it—along with other factors—took me.

Now, as an adult, I realize what a low-rent joke Joey's lifestyle was. But fourteen years ago I wanted to think that my boyfriend was dangerous and that there was something appealing and exciting about life's dark side. Just like in the movies. If Joey had tried that act with a sensible adult woman, she would have just rolled her eyes and walked away.

Joey had a lot of money (well, to a teenager it was a lot of money), and that, along with the fun he offered and the criminal activities he was involved with—or pretended to be involved with—seemed like a great lifestyle to me, a mixed-up kid with screwed-up priorities.

Why work? Why try to achieve goals? Why try to better yourself when you can just commit crimes and have tons of money and a lot of fun?

It's not that these crimes of his (running chop shops and being involved with prostitution and drugs) excited me. It's that I thought that he was adventurous and … a man of danger, so to speak. Little did I know what danger he would lead me toward.

I didn't realize what he really was. He was just a fat, old slob who happened to be nothing more than a common criminal. But at the time I was an immature kid—one who idolized the wrong behavior. Many kids at some point in their teenage years get drunk, try pot, and become sexually active. These are all negative behaviors, but they do it. Why? Because they want to be cool. Combine those behaviors with a troubled, self-centered girl who needed to be loved, like I was, and you have a volatile mixture.

ABOVE:
Angelic me around age 2.

BELOW:
With the Easter Bunny at age 3, in 1978.

LEFT:
My father and I
on Halloween
1979, when I
was 5 years old.

RIGHT:
Halloween, 1979,
with my father.

ABOVE:
Dad and I in February 1980. I was 5
years old.

BELOW:
My mother and I in October of 1980.

RIGHT:
In 1980, at age 6.

LEFT:
I'm all ears at a
children's zoo in 1982,
when I was around 8
years old.

RIGHT:
On my 10th
birthday in 1984.

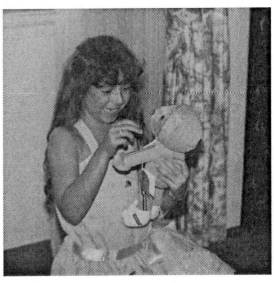

Chapter Three

WHO I WAS

I had a good background. The only child of Rose and Elliot Fisher, I was born and raised in nice communities on Long Island, New York.

I was born on August 21, 1974, in South Nassau Community Hospital in Oceanside, and grew up in Wantagh, on the Island's South Shore, until I was thirteen (a bad age to move). We then relocated to Merrick, to 2092 Berkley Lane. I attended good schools and had nice friends. But what I didn't have was my parents' attention.

When I was young, I used to think that my mother *wanted* to work, that she didn't want to be with me. But the truth was that she hated working and having to wake up early in the morning and leave me. I have since realized that she would have loved nothing more than to stay home with her young daughter and make crafts or just read. But she was a workaholic, and the irony was that she did it to make my life better.

Today I can say that I love my parents, but when I was a kid, I felt like they didn't know anything, and I thought I knew everything.

My parents had this view of me: "She's a good kid. She's a nice girl. She doesn't need our supervision." So my mother went to work. My father, who had a heart attack when I was four years old, remained very nervous about his health; he was around the house all the time and stayed in bed from 1978 to 1986. It wasn't a question of laziness—he just had a mental breakdown, and he was afraid he was going to die.

When I was almost thirteen, I became a latchkey kid. And just as thirteen had been a bad age for me to move, it was also a bad year for me to be left unsupervised. With all that freedom, I just went wild. My parents gave me too much rope to hang myself.

I had been very happy where I had been living in Wantagh. But suddenly I found myself in a new environment—and I mean suddenly. One summer I went on a teen tour throughout the East Coast (ending in Disney World), and when I returned, I learned that my parents had moved us. I was aware that we were going to move, but I didn't really understand what that really entailed, so it was a total surprise to me when it actually happened.

I came back to a new house. I never packed. I never said good-bye to my friends—my best friend had lived next door. I had been very comfortable where I was. My parents were very excited about the move, but for me, I believe that the shocking disorientation contributed to my problems.

My parents were working hard to make a good life for me, but they sacrificed giving attention to me. Although when my mother finally came home from a long day at work, she would sit and watch TV with me and we'd talk or go to the mall, but there really wasn't enough time that she was free. Those rare moments together were special times to me.

I was a really good kid. But whenever there was a rare problem, after the ranting and raving on my father's part, my parents would say, "It's okay, she learned her lesson," and nothing more was ever said. I had never been punished in my life, and I never had constructive discipline like being grounded or losing TV privileges.

By the time I was a teenager, my parents were totally unaware of what I was doing. My mom likes to say I was good at hiding things, but the reality is that I didn't have to hide — there was no one around to catch me. And really, some of the things I was doing were desperate cries. I was calling out for help that I wasn't getting.

My parents just figured that by the time I was a teenager I was practically an adult and knew right from wrong. They just let me do what I wanted to do. I know so many parents now who do the same thing with their teens. Every parent wants to see only the good in their child.

When I was young, before I was a teenager, my father used to beat me for no reason. I think back to some of the few specific things that I got in trouble for, like a bad grade, and the end result would be my parents saying, "Everything's okay now. Don't do it again." I'd get yelled at and hit, but that was it.

But when I got older, I got in more trouble, and again, my parents would say, "We know you're a good kid." So my thinking always was, *Okay, they love me, it's over,* and

I would go on to the next bad thing, although my bad actions were not actively predetermined. I wasn't sitting around saying, "Well, I wonder what bad thing I can do now." I just did the wrong things.

Now I think that if my son did these things, I'd be paying closer attention and he'd be punished. He would not be going out at night. I'd be on his back day and night. Forget it, he would be chained to the bed. But I learned this lesson the hard way, didn't I?

I remember sitting in a prison years later at seventeen years old, thinking, *I'm in here with some really heavy-duty career criminals.*

I thought, *Umm, I'm not sitting in wealthy suburbia anymore, worrying about when I'm going to go to the shopping mall.* And I was looking at these criminals around me, these poor and uneducated people, who never really had a shot at life, and I came to realize how I had squandered my youth and the opportunity I'd had the privilege to have been given.

I would think, *I might belong here because I did something wrong, but emotionally I don't belong here.* I was from a whole different place. I committed an unthinkable criminal act, but I wasn't a habitual criminal who kept going in and out of that place as though I were caught in a revolving door. And I sat there seven years, all by myself, literally, just enclosed in a little shell, reading books, trying to not really speak to people, attempting to figure it all out.

It's hard to just live all by yourself for so many years, emotionally kicking yourself, saying, *How did I end up here?*

I had a whole bunch of people—family, friends, attorneys—saying, "Oh, it's not your fault, it's Joey's fault." And I was sitting there saying to myself, *Well, ya know what? Joey isn't sitting in here in prison next to me. I'm here all by myself, so obviously somebody thinks this is my fault. Prosecutors, people who put me here, they believe I belong here, so why* am *I here?* Once I acknowledged that I was there for a reason and this was my fault, I started to ask: *Okay, how did this happen?*

There were so many warning signs in my past. I am hoping that by reflecting on and writing about my life—some of it very painful—I can help stop others from getting into the same kind of trouble. Who better to tell kids and parents, "These are the warning signs," not spouting them from some textbook but rather from real-life experience? Who better to tell kids, "I did these stupid things, and I'm here to tell you that this is what you should watch out for?"

When I was thirteen, I moved to upscale Merrick from middle-class Wantagh. Merrick's class distinctions were a real problem. They actually separated the school district to keep the exclusive part exclusive, and God pity the economically deprived kids in that small poor pocket of snotty Merrick.

There are three high schools in the Bellmore-Merrick school district: Mepham (in the news recently because of the horrible football "hazing" scandal that became a criminal sexual assault case) is in North Bellmore and is middle-class; Calhoun High, in North Merrick, is also middle-class; and John F. Kennedy High School, where I attended school, combines students from South Merrick and South Bellmore, which are very wealthy. Kennedy was a place where it was a detriment if your father wasn't an oral surgeon or world-class attorney. It was extremely competitive.

About 5 percent of Kennedy's students were considered "poor kids" (in reality they were middle-class), who were therefore not popular and were ostracized. It was disgusting. The rich kids would call them "white trash." How sad. You can't have a normal upbringing in a place like that.

My mother basically bought my popularity (and I wasn't even that popular, just average) — expensive clothes, sports car, teen tours. The credo was: "If so-and-so's parents got it for their kid, then I have to get it for mine."

I had a $20,000 sports car when I was sixteen. Would you do that for your kid? I wouldn't do it for mine. It's crazy. And of course, I never appreciated anything, which is even worse. To this day I call my mother to apologize for my behavior during those years.

I didn't get the exact car I wanted, and I was mad at my parents. What I needed was a good spanking. Living in that community, I was completely out of touch with reality. If I had a kid like I was, with that attitude, it would be unacceptable.

I believe I would never have been like that if I hadn't moved from my sensible middle-class neighborhood. My neighbors there were firemen, police officers, teachers, construction workers — all down-to-earth people who didn't have money to buy their kids things like the teens in Merrick were getting.

It was culture shock.

Every kid in my new school seemed to have a Jaguar or Mercedes. There was a joke that the student parking lot blew away the teachers' parking lot, which was filled with little Toyota Corollas.

Everyone was judged by those material things and not by who they were. While I liked it then, I see now in retrospect that being in that environment was not the way to prepare anyone for the real world.

Even with everything my parents were buying me, it

was still of a minimal level—enough to get by so I wasn't tortured by the other kids. My parents owned a fabric store, where my mother did interior design, and the store created this illusion of wealth, so I was accepted somewhat—enough not to be picked on.

I became moderately popular. I wasn't with the "A" crowd, but I was definitely in the "B" crowd. Every once in a while we got to go to an A-crowd party, though. That was about it.

I had my ten closest friends, and we did everything together—shopping, eating, movies, talking on the phone all day. All our mothers scrambled to get us into the same classes when the schedules were made up. We even went on a trip to California together during the summer when we were fourteen. My mother would tell my father, "She has to go. Her friends are going." So they plopped down the ten grand.

My mother grew up poor and always wanted to give me all the things she never had. She thought it would make me happier, but it never did. I've come to realize that no one is ever fully content with his or her lot in life.

When I was sixteen, I withdrew from all my ten pals, my tight crowd. I didn't stay friends with even one of the gang. I started hanging out with Joey. I started cutting classes at school and hanging out with the other kids who cut classes and were considered rebels or outsiders but in reality were kids destined for Loser Central. I didn't fit in with the smoking, drinking crowd with no life ambition, but I hung out with them anyway. That didn't last long.

I then drifted toward girls who were older than me. Girls who were friends with an ex-boyfriend of mine, who had just graduated from high school, from Mepham and Calhoun—not the rich, snobby girls. We had been at the same places many times, so we knew each other, but at the end of the night we always went back to our very different lives.

These were nice middle-class girls with jobs. Some were attending community college. Their boyfriends worked construction jobs or in pizzerias. These girls were two to three years older than I was. They were very into the nightclub scene. Their clothes were nice, sexy, and came from the mall, not from the trendy boutiques we shopped at where I lived. There was nothing wrong with this; in fact, most people lived in their world, not the one I was living in.

Their world was the real world, and I found it attractive. Again, the warning signs were there for my parents: change in friends, slipping grades, staying out late. With my old friends I went shopping and to the movies, and I'd be home by 11:30 P.M. With these new friends I wasn't even leaving the house to go out until 11:30 P.M.

Looking back, I can see there was something terribly troublesome going on in my head. I remember missing my Merrick friends. I wanted desperately to turn the clock back, but I couldn't. I wanted to act grown-up. I acted older. I went to nightclubs. I withdrew. I tossed my old gang aside like they didn't matter. How could I say, "I miss you, you guys are my whole life?" I just couldn't, and I was miserable, pretending I liked my new life on the wild side. I was more receptive to the world around Joey's body shop than the trendy stores my old friends would frequent.

Joey fit in perfectly with my plan to act all grown-up, and hanging out with him was a complement to my new group of older friends. He brought me into an adult world that was appealing for a little while, but once I realized I didn't have my best old buddies to share it with, well, it just became a sad place to be.

When my Merrick girlfriends heard about Joey, instead of being excited for me, they recoiled in disgust, so I started gravitating more toward people like Joey. I felt that nobody understood me. My friends would say, "Ugh. He's old and he works in a body shop." I was in a very confused place—I wanted the material things, but I was still rebelling against the lifestyle.

The truth was that I was raised in a different world from Joey and the new kids I was hanging out with. I was different, but I was trying to pretend I was just like them. I didn't know who I was at that point. And that feeling has been a running theme in my life.

My parents developed a good business, and I was raised in a very affluent community. What people didn't know was that I lived in a place that my parents had worked hard to attain. They had scraped and sacrificed to move into this neighborhood that was basically the 90210 of New York.

In Merrick I never felt as good as the other girls. I was happy in Wantagh, where I was a regular kid—on the softball team, not obsessed about clothes, makeup, and manicures. I think that by hanging out with this new blue-collar crowd and leaving my more privileged friends behind, I was trying to recapture that happiness.

It's funny. Although my parents strove for a good life, they were very frugal, because they wanted to be able to afford to raise me in a place like Merrick so I would get the best education possible. They felt that wealthier people educated their children better. They wanted one of the best school districts in New York, and they hoped that I'd go on to a great Ivy League college and be a doctor or attorney someday. They never dreamed I'd be the Long Island Lolita because I moved there. Had they known, I'm sure they would have stayed in a middle-class neighborhood. Probably I would have stayed trouble-free in Wantagh, but had I gotten in trouble there and been arrested, everyone would have said, "Yeah, it happens. There are plenty of girls who get arrested on Long Island. She's not the only one." The media just wouldn't have cared.

But the media did care. They like it when rich people go bad. But in this case their perception that I was wealthy was incorrect. That's the whole point—my parents owned a small business. The irony was that my mother used to scrape her money together to buy her jeans on sale, and she'd clip out coupons for the supermarket so we could afford to move into this new upscale Merrick neighborhood. She did it with all these admirable intentions, and I screwed it all up. The media hopped on it like my father was a neurosurgeon making $6 million a year. And it just wasn't true.

My mother and I were always close, but she was always too nice. No matter what bad thing happened or what bad thing anyone did, she would always look for the bright spot. She never yelled at me. My mother doesn't yell. She doesn't know how to yell. My father was very different—he always yelled. In fact, when my father screamed at my mother, she used to cry. She is a straight arrow. She never smoked, never drank, never did anything wrong. She did everything she was supposed to do, and she believed that since she was like that, I would be like that. Moms out there, are you listening?

Being a teenager is hard even under the best conditions. Beautiful girls feel ugly; smart girls feel stupid. It's just the nature of the beast. Insecurities run rampant during those years. I can only guess that I was a casualty of changing from child to adult too quickly. The natural progression sped up when I met Joey.

I was a really nice girl when I was young. All my teachers would tell that to my parents. I always did well in school. I played soccer. But then when things went sour, they degenerated pretty quickly. I was a pretty good student until my grades started going downhill in tenth grade, and by eleventh grade I was practically failing. My senior year was a total disaster. Guess when I started dating Joey?

I remember as a teen having so many questions about sex and relationships and being afraid to ask my mother. Not afraid that I would be punished, but afraid that she would think I was strange or that something was wrong with me. So instead I would ask my friends. It never dawned on me that they were also afraid to ask their parents and knew no more than I did.

My mother was adamant about me being "good." She warned me to never go beyond kissing. The thought of asking my mother about sex was horrifying.

When I was in the sixth grade, my mother and I went to my school one evening for a program on sex. All the other sixth-grade girls were there with their mothers. A movie on body development was shown. I think every girl in that room wanted to curl up and just die. At the end we were given a pamphlet on reproduction, and our mothers were instructed to go home and read it with us. My mother obediently complied. She read the pamphlet to me and asked if I had any questions. NO, I didn't have any questions. Well, not for Mom anyway.

No matter how nice our mothers are, we still don't want to discuss sex with them. Even now at thirty, married with a child, I still can't discuss sex with my mother. I can talk about anything else, just not the "S" word.

Had I only been more comfortable with my mother, my life would have been dramatically different. If you're a teenage girl reading this book and you're caught up in something you should not be caught up in, please take my advice. Talk to your mother or another responsible grown-up. You see how the silence, the embarrassment, led to something much worse with me. One conversation could have probably put the world right.

Had I been able to talk to my mother, she would have stopped my relationship with Joey. She would have gone and knocked on Joey's door and talked to his wife. If she had done that, I would have been humiliated and I would have hated her, but Joey would have never come near me again. My mother would have gone to the district attorney, and Joey would have been arrested right there and then for statutory rape.

My father was a different story than my mother. He would beat the hell out of me. If he had not been in the picture, my life would have been very different. I lived with the constant fear of violence, the fear that he would hurt me. I never told my mother anything because she wouldn't have been able to keep it to herself and she would have confronted him, and I'd have been in more trouble.

I was never close to my father. He could be really nice and funny at times, but he had a trigger temper. He was so strict, and I didn't want any rules. I didn't want to listen. My mother was completely the opposite and not strict at all. She kept saying about me, "Let her be who she's going to be." She was one of those flower children from the '60s. My mother loved me too much. She was blind to my faults.

If I did anything wrong, my mother would run to the bookstore and get some child psychology book. She didn't believe in any corporal punishment, and she felt that a child should never be made to feel bad. On the other hand, my father was very abusive. Usually, when I did something wrong (it was always little things like spilling juice on the table), by the time my mother arrived home my father had already handled it his way. Looking back at it, if there had been a happy medium between their opposite child-rearing approaches (if my mother had been less good-natured and my father less abusive), I wouldn't have gotten into so much trouble later on.

I'd come home from school at 3:00 P.M. and was alone with my father until 6:00 P.M. every weekday, and all day Saturdays. I remember sitting by my window and praying that my mother would come home, because once she was home my father's abuse would stop.

I spent my childhood not knowing that he smacked my mother around, and she spent that time not knowing he was doing the same thing to me. She could have endured it herself, but had she known he was abusing me, she would have left him on the spot. But nobody ever talked about it.

Things were so bad with my father that at age eleven I ran away from home with my seven-year-old cousin. We didn't get far—we were only gone about three hours, and only made it to a few towns away. When the police found us wandering the streets, they brought us home, and my mother was so happy to see me that she kept kissing me and said she couldn't understand why I wanted to run away. My father didn't say anything until the next day when I came home from school and he started screaming at me and smacking me around, demanding to know if I had told my mother about the things he was doing to me.

There was nothing positive in the way he dealt with me; in fact, I don't recall him ever saying he loved me. He just beat me up. That is not the way to raise a child. It got to the point where he didn't want to listen to my mother, who wanted to handle things in a more civilized way. It was easier for him to just say, "Do what you want," and slam the door rather than try to discipline me properly. Then he would have me crying and trying to do what I wanted anyway, and my mother sitting and crying all night because he was so abusive and horrible. Keep in mind that I was a well-behaved child and that the things he would be so angry about were minor, like having a messy room or not being able to answer a spontaneous math question that he insisted I should know the answer to.

I started to withdraw and became very quiet, always trying to be good and keep out of his way, like a typical abused child. But when I became a teenager, I just rebelled and turned wild.

My father was very violent throughout my childhood. I knew even as a little kid that it was abuse, because all little kids get scared of that sort of thing. Now I don't ever hit my son, because I remember that terrible fear of getting hit when I was young.

My father was always yelling at me, hitting me, slapping me, pulling me, pushing me, and grabbing my arms. And then he'd grab me and hug me and make me kiss him. I'd recoil. Kids want playmates, even in their parents, but I wanted nothing to do with him.

My father had been married prior to his marriage to my mother and had an adopted daughter with his first wife. They got divorced because they said he was so abusive to them, and after a while they had absolutely nothing to do with him. The girl was around twelve at that time. They just wanted him out of their lives. My mother never really believed their stories at the beginning, thinking they were generated by a scorned wife spewing accusations from an angry divorce. Little did she know that I would end up living that girl's life and she would end up living the life of the ex-wife.

He was always on my back. When I did my homework he would stand over me, and if I got something wrong he would yell and make me say the answers over and over again, just repeat the correct answers. So I learned to tell him that I either didn't have homework or had already done it.

He was such a nitpicker that after a while I started doing all my homework after bedtime by nightlight. When I came home from school, no one would ever check. I did it in the solitude of my room so that he wouldn't know and wouldn't bother me about it.

He tortured me about everything. He wanted me to do well, but he was so misdirected that he didn't know how to go about it.

He would tell people how wonderful and beautiful I was, but alone with me he would tell me I was horrible. If I played baseball with the other kids, he would take me aside and say, "Why can't you be like those kids?" And then he'd give me a whole list of what I was doing wrong. Instead of playing catch with me, he would lecture me for ten minutes on one throw.

Once I had a school project where we had to make something out of construction paper to indicate what we wanted to be when we grew up. I wanted to be a lawyer. When he saw the project, he said, "You're not smart enough. You'll never be a lawyer." He made me feel so bad. Inadequate. I was about nine years old.

One day I came home and my father had ransacked my bedroom. Everything was thrown on the floor. I didn't say anything to him, and he didn't say anything to me. When my mother came home and asked him what had happened, he said that my room was a mess, so he decided to teach me a lesson. How did my mother handle it? She bought me a lock for the bedroom. Instead of addressing the issue, she placed a lock on my bedroom door.

I was terrified of my father. He continuously hit me until I was about thirteen. Once I became a teenager, he didn't really hit me anymore, but the abuse was still there. And the fear was still there, so all he had to do was raise his voice and I was terrified.

The end of the physical abuse did not end the fear that had been drilled into me throughout my young life. My father never stopped screaming and throwing things. I would hear his loud, thumping footsteps walking toward my bedroom, and my heart would start beating uncontrollably. I was terrified. I was never sure when his mind would snap and he would fly into one of his sudden rages.

Sometime early in my sixteenth year my father flew into one of his ranting fits. It was because my room was a mess. He was knocking everything off my dresser, throwing my belongings all around the room. He was a screaming lunatic, as he had been so many times before that I had lost count. This time was different. He started grabbing me, slapping me, yelling at the top of his lungs. I was terrified, but unlike during my childhood, when I would sit there and take the abuse, I ran. I got away from him and managed to run out of my house.

It was cold out; I had no shoes, no coat. I just ran. I didn't care. I was tired of the abuse. I remember running through my backyard and the neighbor's bushes with no destination in mind. I was cold and scared. Finally, when I was a few blocks away, I was crying and trying to think what to do, where to go. One of my girlfriends lived up the block. I went to her house. She asked me what I was doing and where my shoes were.

"What is wrong with you?" she asked.

Embarrassed, I told her I had gone outside and accidentally gotten locked out of my house. I asked her if I could wait at her house till my parents came home. I really just needed some time to think about things. I didn't want to go home.

By sixteen, I hated my father and was forever dreaming of the day I could get away from him forever.

I called my aunt and told her what had happened. She knew what my father was like, and she felt terrible for me. She let me stay with her for a few days. During this time my parents had no idea where I was. They called the police to file a missing person report. My father apparently went off on one of his tirades while filling out the report, spewing about how awful I was, incorrigible, uncontrollable.

After several weeks my mother begged me to come home. I went with her because I didn't know what else to do. I was a kid; I had no way to escape life with my father.

When I was arrested in 1992, Nassau County Assistant District Attorney Fred Klein used this police report as a tool to say I would flee if granted bail. After all, my own loving father had called me incorrigible and uncontrollable. So my bail was set at a whopping $2 million.

I was eventually released on bail, and guess what? I didn't flee. I often wonder if it ever dawned on Prosecutor Klein or Judge Marvin Goodman, the judge who presided over my case, that I couldn't flee if released on bail, no matter how high or low it was, because I had nowhere to run. Just as I'd had nowhere to run the previous year when I tried to escape my father's wrath.

The last time I saw my father was in 1993 when I was in prison. He always requested to visit me in prison, but I wouldn't let him except for that one time. I had endured too many years of being hit and screamed at and being terrified. He tortured me.

While I was in prison, he wrote letters to me every week. I threw them out. He would say he was sorry, but I was too angry. If he had lived longer, after I was released and had a son and straightened out my life, it would have worked out between us. I lacked the maturity to overcome it back then, though.

For every one rant, there would be twenty good things he would do. He was 90 percent a nice guy. We tend to forget the good and remember the bad. But the bad was bad.

He was also abusive to my mother.

Once, when I was fourteen, I came into their room and he was on top of her, choking her. She was all bruised. After that, I would constantly think, why is she still with him?

She went to my aunt, and my aunt and my grandmother took pictures as evidence. My father voluntarily went to a hospital and checked himself into the psych ward. I was excited because I thought my mother was going to leave him. I was so thrilled. But she had been set to leave him a thousand times before. He came back home and they reconciled.

It has taken time for me to realize that not only was I abused, but I was also a victim of the domestic violence perpetrated against my mother.

When I ask my mother, "Why didn't you leave?" she says she was frightened. In the 1970s and '80s domestic violence was not thought of the way it is today. It was unheard of. No one talked about it. Not until November 1987, when Greenwich Village lawyer Joel Steinberg killed his six-year-old daughter Lisa, and the world saw the broken, beaten face of his wife, Hedda Nussbaum.

People started to realize the importance and seriousness of domestic abuse and child abuse when they realized it was a crime that knew no class or racial boundaries. That was a huge turning point in America.

Sometimes I thought that, despite his nuttiness and abuse, my father loved me and in the long run he would take care of me. That was one of the appeals of Joey. I was looking for an adult to take care of me.

But my father had problems till the end. When my parents separated in 1992, my father tortured my mother throughout the divorce proceedings.

During those proceedings, my father, who didn't want the divorce, was bitter. He tried everything to get back with her. He would call constantly, sometimes twenty times a night, until my mother had to take her phone off the hook. He would try to be nice and understanding, begging her to try marriage again. When she refused, he would become enraged, vicious, and she would hang up on him. Then in the next call he would apologize, again begging for forgiveness, and the cycle would start again. This went on for a few years. It actually was just a different stage of their turbulent twenty-year marriage, but without the physical abuse.

During divorce proceedings people need to come to agreement on the issues, but my father disagreed on every point, just to be difficult and prolong the process. That's why, after being separated for eight years, they still weren't divorced. He spent his last years clinging to the hope that he would get back together with my mother.

Before my father forced the sale of our Merrick house, he had already moved out, but my mom was still living there. He would break into the house and take out items that he knew meant something to her. She finally got creative and put fish tanks under all the windows so he would fall into them when he broke in. Eventually he stopped doing it.

When the house was sold, my mother bought a condo. He would stand outside and stare up at her windows. He would wait for her to come out.

My father passed away on Easter Day 2000. It was a year after I was released. My parents were obviously no longer together (they never ended up officially divorced), and I was living on my own in an apartment in Long Beach. I hadn't seen him since 1993, and I wanted to see him when I got out of prison. I wanted to have an adult relationship with him. I just felt I needed some time first to get my head together. And suddenly I got the call telling me that he had died.

Chapter Four

THE BIG QUESTION: WHY?

A ll these experiences were answers to the question I would be asking myself in prison:

Why?

I still don't know all the whys, but once I began asking the question, I said to myself, *Okay, I did X, Y, and Z, and these were horrible things, and I don't want to do these things anymore*, and I made a conscious decision to try to be a better, more compassionate human being. I had a lot of time to reflect, and there was a lot of time for self-discovery and self-healing. That and the natural maturing process.

I came to realize that I was very into what men thought. You know what? If Joey told me to do something, even if I didn't want to do it I did it anyway, because I was so insecure and immature that I did it to please him. Can you imagine? I did things against my own nature for another person, forgetting about my own happiness and my own needs and the well-being of others, because all that was irrelevant. But in jail, when I was sitting there by myself, my own personal needs, my survival, became more important.

That helped me, because when I was released from prison and I started dating men and they would say, "I'll pick you up at eight o'clock," and didn't show up, well, that was the end of that. When I was a teenager, if my date would say, "I'm sorry," and then stand me up, I'd say, "Okay," and I would go out with him the next day.

I learned to put limits on what I will and will not accept. That made me a very lonely person for a little while, but a stronger person in the long run.

There is no question that it was my interaction with men that got me into such trouble. And my view of men has definitely changed over the years. I still love men, but I only like the nice ones now. I don't like the bad ones anymore. Also, now that I'm not a teenager, I've learned it's better to love only one at a time.

A lot of the things I went through in prison changed me as a person. A lot of the abuse that I suffered in prison made me recognize the abuse I inflicted on Mary Jo, and her pain. When you go through pain of your own, you realize and appreciate somebody else's.

It's not that I didn't know right from wrong. I did. I knew shooting somebody was wrong. I just did not care. I was oblivious.

Somehow violence was very, very cool to me. And for the life of me, I don't know why I did it. I'll never have an answer for that. I look as an adult now at what I did as a teenager, totally separated from that time, and I see that there is no logical reason for why I did it. I have no idea, other than that I wanted to impress Joey. I wanted to be cool, I wanted to be loved, and I didn't understand that what I did was a horrific thing that ruined many lives. I didn't realize that somebody could be wiped off the face of the Earth, that what I did could actually physically affect another person. It was all about me. And that's the biggest thing: when you can't see anyone outside yourself and your own needs, that's when problems arise. So I didn't think about this woman having two small beautiful children. My God, as a mother now, when I think that someone would take away my little boy's mother … it's just the worst. But at that time it never entered my mind, because mentally I was a child myself. It was just terrible.

Joey would say, "Want to shoot my wife for me?"

And then he'd say, "Oh, I'm just kidding, I'll do it myself."

But you know, when someone keeps repeating something over and over again and then compounding it by saying it to an impressionable mixed-up kid, it has an effect.

He would cry, "Oh, if I end up in jail, will you miss me?" And of course I didn't want him to end up in jail. And he would say, "Oh, you're just a kid. I'll protect you and nothing will happen to you. They don't put kids in jail."

So as far as I knew, kids couldn't go to jail, and I didn't want anything to happen to him, so I thought, *If I do this and I'm protecting him, he's not going to go to jail and he'll be happy.* How pathetic was that? I wanted *him* to be happy. Forget about *my* whole life and my future and Mary Jo and her children and her parents. As long as *he* was happy…and in return, if he was happy, then I would derive happiness from his happiness, because I had no identity of my own.

I thought it was a good idea because I was susceptible to his supposed kindness and I was having this "romance" with him. He was the first adult male I was ever with. Before him it had been just teenage boys. So I listened to him.

I was used to dealing with adults (parents, aunts, uncles, teachers) in a certain way because I had been brought up to believe that when an adult tells you something, you believe them. You believe and do what they tell you. Your teachers tell you something, and you just say, okay, and you do it, whether you like it or not. They know everything. So if an adult, an authority figure, told me something, I thought he knew what he was talking about. I just thought whatever Joey said was what I should do. He knew what I was going to do in regard to Mary Jo, and he didn't stop me.

I think he was probably just blown away when he got that phone call, thinking, *Oh my God, she really did it.*

There was no real planning. Getting the gun was so easy. I could have gotten a gun on the street in five minutes. I met this kid Peter Guagenti, and I basically just said, "Can I have your gun?" And he just said, "Oh, okay," and that was it.

He was from Brooklyn. At that time it seemed like you could walk to any street corner in Brooklyn and just say, "I need a piece," and someone would say, "Sure," and that was it. It's ridiculous how easy it was.

Once I got the gun, I remember Joey begging, "Oh, let me see it, let me see it."

I said, "I don't have it with me."

He responded by taunting me, "You don't have it," as if I were making it up.

Now I think maybe he thought that I was just trying to impress him. I was a goofy kid, and I was listening, hanging on his every word. I think back and say, *Oh my God, how could I have done this?* And it took many years for me to come to the point I'm at now.

I feel like a totally different person today. I look back and don't even know who that person was back then. I watch all those biographies and news programs and I get sick, because I see my picture and I know it was me, but that's not me. And I just want to be in denial, thinking that's not me. It's really hard. But it *was* me.

Chapter Five

MEETING JOEY

One fateful meeting often changes a person's life. A lifelong friend. A teacher who inspires. A networking moment that turns into a career. But my one fateful meeting changed many lives.

I want to write about my time with Joey. I really want that experience to be as helpful to other young girls as it can be. But part of my memory is gone. I think subconsciously I blocked out large portions of this time period because it was the root of the pain and troubles that ultimately led to my crime and incarceration. But what I do remember is as clear as anything.

Another thing I can tell you is that the stories about this time, whether they were books, movies, or news articles, really lay Joey and my love story on thick. But it just wasn't true. I now know he didn't love me. It was built up as a great romance, but it was a romance in my head.

I do know he used me, obviously for sexual gratification and to boost his middle-aged ego. I would speculate that I made him feel young, and it was probably amusing to him that I did anything he said, as if I were his own personal windup doll.

When I was around fifteen years old, he did auto repair work for my father. I was probably in his shop, Complete Auto Body in Baldwin, a half-dozen times. One day I was walking around his shop while my father spoke with him. Joey didn't know that I was with my father. He saw me and turned to my father and said, "Look at that girl. Look at her ass. She's so hot."

My father was understandably shocked and angry, and he said, "That's my daughter. She's fifteen." Joey apologized.

On Halloween 1990, I had only had my car for a month. I parked it at school, and the entire car was egged. They had jumped on the hood and covered it in shaving cream. We brought it to Complete Auto Body. Joey was very nice to me. He joked around with me and started talking about music while we sat in his office. He asked me if he should put pin-striping on it.

"It's expensive," I said.

"Don't worry, I'll talk to your father," he told me and winked.

He was so nice to me. Little did I know how that meeting would change my whole life.

One morning in May 1991, I was late for school. I was tired, and I ended up backing up out of the garage sideways, and I smashed the side of my car, knocking the whole electric mirror off. I panicked because I knew my father would take the car away from me.

I called Rob, my boyfriend at the time, and we got a couple of quotes from body shops for a couple of thousand dollars. That amount of money for the repair was way beyond my reach. I remembered how nice Joey had been to me, and I thought that I should go in and talk to him. I thought he was just a nice old guy who would help.

I went in and asked for him, and I'll never forget how kind he was. Instead of looking right at my car, he asked me, "How are you doing? Would you like to get something to eat?" He kept telling me to calm down. I was hyperventilating.

He finally took a look at the car and said, "Yeah, it's a lot of damage." He couldn't fix it up for me right there. So he gave me an exact script for what I should say to my father so it would match the damage.

He told me to say I parked the car at a mall, and we would say the accident occurred there. I thought he was so cool for helping me out. My father believed the plausible story.

"This is the only way this could have happened," Joey explained to him. He fixed the car, and my father paid for it.

When we returned home, my father was standing outside, in front of the garage door, which Rob had just sanded and repainted. My father was ranting and raving (as usual) about how horrible the drivers were in the mall parking lot, and he was leaning up against the freshly painted door. When he walked away from us toward the house, his entire back was covered with paint. I threw his clothes in the garbage later that day. He never knew.

Part of the problem was that I wasn't the best driver. I was sixteen. A month and a half after that mirror incident, on the way to summer school, I took a shortcut through a gas station to avoid a red light. As I drove through the station at forty miles per hour I ran over an old gas pump on the ground, which pulled out the whole undercarriage.

Who should I go to for help? Well, Joey Buttafuoco, of course. He had been so helpful before.

When I called Joey, he said, "If I didn't know any better, I would think you're doing this just to see me."

I was completely hysterical. He came to the gas station and looked at the car. He called my father and told him someone had cut me off. He lied and fixed the problem. Again. In my eyes he was a hero. Now can you see why at sixteen years old I thought he was the coolest thing on Earth? He was fixing all my problems for me.

Complete Auto Body was located about ten minutes away from home. My father dropped me off to pick the car up after Joey had been working on it, and ended up leaving me there. The car wasn't ready, and Joey said to me, "Don't call your father, I'll drive you home."

So that's how it started.

It was afternoon, and Joey drove me home. It was July 2, 1991. When we got to my house, he asked, "Aren't you gonna invite me in?" It was the middle of the day, and my parents were working. I invited him in, and I did all the polite things, offering him something to drink, showing him around. I told him about the large fish tank in my bedroom, and he wanted to see it.

You know what? I thought he actually wanted to see my fish tank. I thought he was being just a really nice guy. Obviously he wasn't interested in the fish tank—he was interested in my bedroom.

Upstairs in my bedroom, before I knew it, he threw me on the bed and began telling me how much he loved me and how I was all he had been thinking about for months. I was experiencing a dizzy feeling listening to all these nice things he was saying. It was good. I was in a state of shock.

"Don't worry, I had a vasectomy," he said to me. But that wasn't something a sixteen-year-old has on her mind. I wasn't even sure what a vasectomy was.

We had sex, and he kept saying all these really sweet things to me. I was kind of sheltered. I had only had one real boyfriend before this. Teenagers don't know about casual sex. My thinking was, *Okay, Joey, we had sex, now you're my boyfriend.* He was doing boyfriend things.

Afterward I called my girlfriends—and their reaction was incredibly negative: "That's horrible." "He's too old." "No, no, no, no. That's disgusting." Even at sixteen, my friends knew it was not normal. And I thought it was.

For me, it was simple. Simple. I like you. You like me. We did this, now we're involved.

At first I didn't know he was married. He never wore a ring. I never even thought he'd be married. I was incredibly naïve. My parents wouldn't behave like that. I thought that once people were married they stopped dating. When my parents had a fight, they didn't sleep with someone else—my father went and hung out at Dunkin Donuts all night.

Later that day, after we had sex in my bedroom, he called me from work to tell me how wonderful I made him feel, that I made him feel so special.

He asked me if he could take me to dinner and a movie. That night I told my parents that I was going out with friends and that they were picking me up down the street. How could they ever have imagined what was really going on? I was living it and I could hardly comprehend it.

He brought me to a really nice restaurant. Remember, I was a teenager. A date had never taken me to any place beyond a pizzeria. The only other time I had been in such a nice place was on my parents' anniversary.

He must really like me to take me to a place like this, I thought.

After the restaurant, no movie as promised. We went straight to a hotel.

The next day he told me he was married.

"Why are you with me?" I asked him.

"I want to get divorced," he told me. "I'm unhappy." How was I to know that these were the same lines every cheater tells his girlfriend?

Joey had a knack for making me feel very special, which really didn't mean much considering how young, vulnerable, and easily manipulated I was. Later, after I was arrested, an investigator hired by my lawyer found numerous other women with whom Joey was involved. Each one said that he made her feel like she was the only person on Earth. The Nassau County police detectives also came up with other women Joey was seeing when they went through his motel receipts with me.

The flirting process with Joey started at fifteen, and at sixteen I became sexually involved with him. How does someone that young and troubled handle a Joey Buttafuoco? I look back and shudder thinking how young I was. Sixteen. Do you remember when you were sixteen?

If you have a sixteen-year-old involved with a twenty-year-old guy, that's one thing, but a girl who is sixteen and a man in his mid-thirties … that's not normal. It's not legal. And shockingly enough, that did not sink into my thick skull until recently.

My friends would say to me, "You're with a pervert," and again, I was so under his spell that I would just think that *they* were stupid. I would say that they weren't as "mature" as I was. Can you imagine! It wasn't until I grew up that I realized how wrong it was, and how manipulated I was.

One day last year I called my editor, Robbie Woliver, at the *Long Island Press*. We were working on a cover story I was writing about Joey, now forty-seven, who had just been arrested for insurance fraud, on December 17, 2003, in California. (Long Island's loss is California's gain.)

The story was a big exclusive, the first time I discussed Joey in public, and it was my opportunity to examine his current life—drugs, arrests, solicitation of a prostitute, working in the porn business, dating hookers, broken parole, insurance fraud—and compare it to my current life—married with a child, working a respectable job, trying to make sense out of my past and use that experience to help others.

When I got out on parole in 1999, Joey brazenly told the press: "You haven't heard the end of Amy Fisher," as if I were about to newly embark on a life of crime. My ability to show the reality of our lives and who we were and how we both turned out was indeed sweet revenge.

Robbie and I were also working on this book, so a lot of inner reflection was going on. When I called him that day, I blurted out, "It just struck me. Joey was a child molester!" Robbie was dumbfounded by this sudden recognition, as many of you readers might be. While it had been evident to many outsiders for so many years, it took twelve years for it to become evident to me. Better late than never, though.

Here in New York, when an adult has sex with a child under the age of consent—seventeen—it is statutory rape, even if the sex is consensual. The underlying premise is that children under the age of seventeen do not have full capability and understanding and cannot give consent.

I had no experience to fall back on when I was a teenager. If I were single now and I went on a date with a man who took me to dinner and suggested we go to a hotel, dinner would be cut short, there would be no hotel, and the date would end there.

Joey spent only four months in jail for my statutory rape. That, of course, happened only after I was raked through the coals for being the biggest slut in the country. I was sixteen! Where were the women's groups or children's advocates? They quietly grumbled about me being a victim, but it was only after many years, when their agendas were a little less politically sensitive and the tabloid media had calmed down a bit, that they came out to support me in droves. Gee, thanks. (Madonna, however, ripped up a photo of Joey on *Saturday Night Live*, stating, "Fight the real enemy!")

Joey was a sexual predator. That is what he was. And he should have been put in jail for years. He should have been made to feel that there would be consequences for his actions. But he never was, and that's why he's still committing crimes.

It took me all this time to realize that, although much of the world already knew it. In today's climate, perhaps the media would have been more sympathetic to the sixteen-year-old who was also a victim.

But to the media back then, the fact that I was a schoolgirl by day and at night I was hanging out with a married thirty-six-year-old auto mechanic with two kids was tabloid dynamite. Joey, my boyfriend, who was a semi-recovering cocaine addict, was caught up in a life of crime. He ran in shady circles, and alas, I started running in those same circles.

The media went wild with the "crazy teen" stories. Can you imagine better fodder than a teenage seductress for a sensation-hungry media? Added to everything else, I was now a seventeen-year-old call girl.

It was all me, of course. The media made it seem like someone could just live a lifestyle like that without the guidance of an adult. As if a girl could just walk into an escort service at sixteen, on her own, and get a job. It was absurd, but the distorted media version made a lot more money for the networks than the actual events.

You have to know somebody and be in those circles to get a job like an escort. It's not a job at McDonald's — they have to trust you to keep their sordid illegal secrets. And how do they trust you? You have to be recommended and brought in by someone they know. And who in the world do you think brought me into this nightmare world? Yep, you got it. Joey Buttafuoco. Probably the second-worst thing Joey got me involved with was prostitution. At the age of seventeen!

There came a point when Joey recommended that I make my own money. He suggested the ABBA Escort Service, which was run by a friend of his and located around the corner from Complete Auto Body in Baldwin. At this time Joey was spouting a philosophy to explain to me how a married man could have an affair. He kept saying, "You have sex with your body and not with your mind." He was setting me up for this line of work.

"You're beautiful," he would tell me. "Put on the right clothes, look older. Just go out to dinner with these guys and talk to them. They'll pay you just for your company." That doesn't sound so bad, right?

I had never even heard of these things. I knew about prostitutes — those were the women who walked up and down Forty-second Street in Spandex and got paid for having sex with strangers. That's not what an escort was.

He kept trying to convince me to work as an escort. Oh God, was I stupid.

"You'll make money for nothing," Joey said. "A couple of hundred dollars and dinner."

I thought, *Okay.* I didn't think to ask any further questions. I never even met the woman who ran the escort service, Lorraine Wurzburg. I worked for her on Joey's say-so.

In mid-September 1991, two weeks after I turned seventeen, Joey got me work with ABBA Escort Service.

The first time they sent me to go out with a man—Richard—they told him my age. He was about fifty. It turned out he had been a friend-client for thirty years, and he would break me in. He was the "tester."

Richard owned a machinery business on Long Island, in Garden City. After a nice dinner in a posh restaurant, he took me back to his business. He showed me around and tried to kiss me. I told him, "Don't do that!" He took my hand and put it on his crotch and said, "This is what you're getting paid for."

Although we did not have sexual intercourse, the activity escalated in degrees. I felt pressured and cornered. When it was over, I went back to Joey, crying and embarrassed, but I wasn't going to tell him what had happened. I thought that he would look down on me or that he would think I was promiscuous. But I couldn't keep it in and I eventually spilled my guts.

And how did he comfort me?

He said, "It's okay. How much money did you get?"

Every time I complained after that, he repeated the same mantra: "You have sex with your body and not with your mind."

After I was arrested, I learned that he was getting a cut of the money ABBA made on me. And he planned it from day one. He knew everything.

I believed in him. I never would have imagined he would set me up that way. But this was just another part of him whittling away my essence and destroying my self-esteem so that I would have no sense of myself. I was his puppet. I was disintegrating. And he was making money off of my destruction.

As events escalated out of my control that first night, my escort business experience also spun out of control. It became something I just couldn't get away from. I had no mind of my own by this time. I did whatever Joey wanted the little Amy puppet to do. I just could not get out of it, and after a few months I complained to Joey again and told him I wanted to stop. He got nasty and threatened to tell my father.

That was how he controlled me, by blackmailing me. So I kept doing it. I only worked for them for six months, twice a week, at night. I felt dirty. I felt horrible. I didn't want to be touched. I was so depressed. I kept telling Joey that I didn't want to do it.

"Yes, you will," he would tell me. I never even thought to ask why he cared so much about what I did and didn't do.

I was his property, and he got a commission, though I was unaware of it at the time. This guy didn't love me. I'd be surprised if he ever felt anything.

Young girls want to be in love and have a boyfriend and go to the movies and have fun together, not do that sort of thing. I didn't need the money. I wasn't a drug addict trying to support a habit. I wanted love and affection. I wanted to know someone cared. At the beginning, I also wanted to impress and please Joey. Toward the end he coerced me into continuing. He stole my youth away from me. I felt like the saddest girl on Earth.

The real deal: I was a teenager who was seduced by a sleazy, experienced older man. I fell for all the cheesy lines. I fell for all the false, insincere promises. I ate up all the lies as if his words came straight from the Bible. Before Joey, I had only had one boyfriend since I was thirteen. He was also an inexperienced teenager. That was the extent of my worldly experience.

I did things that Joey asked me to do because I thought I loved him and I didn't want him to stop loving me. I was insecure, and I didn't have the life experience to realize that he was either sick or just using me, or both.

People are always shocked that the Nassau County police did nothing to Joey in terms of the prostitution. They never went after anyone. My theory: Nassau County did not value women at all.

Everyone was focused on the media whirlwind and the sensational stories it spewed—and I was the focus of that attention. To the media it was a real-life near-*Fatal Attraction* story. A scorned temptress flips out and shoots her boyfriend's wife in the face. (Just to set that horrible image straight, Mary Jo was not shot in the face, it was in her neck—not that shooting her anywhere was right.) The media lies kept coming. Actually, many of the stories alleged that Joey wasn't even my boyfriend at all and that I imagined the whole thing because I was delusional.

It's not every day that a teenager from an affluent suburb, a girl with no chemical dependencies, works for an escort service. (At least not before the Heidi Fleiss scandal.) The media had a field day with this. Since I didn't need the money, I must have been a nymphomaniac. And even if I wasn't, well, the sex angle made for a better story than the misguided-teen angle.

The media went wild combining a little truth with a lot of fiction to create a sensational story. I wanted to defend myself, to say something, anything. My lawyer, Eric Naiburg, and my parents wouldn't allow me to do so. My lawyer was afraid I would say something that would get me in even more trouble than I was already in. I guess it wasn't obvious to him that with every tabloid article that ran, the public thought I was even crazier than I was. My parents, who always followed the rules in life, listened to the lawyer, never thinking to deviate from his advice.

Even now, still dubbed the Long Island Lolita, I'm seen by some as a promiscuous, unstable teen who shoots her boyfriends' wives. But remember, the book *Lolita* was about a pedophile.

Oh, and Joey's recent paper-shuffling insurance fraud? In March 2004, he got a year for that. Four months served for statutory rape and one year for insurance fraud? What kind of message does that send to young girls and predatory men?

And Joey wasn't just any sexual predator. He was one with a wife who was in the way.

He often talked about getting rid of her. It escalated from his complaints about her being an annoyance to him to the idea of shooting her. And he'd repeat that they don't put kids in jail.

He didn't say, "Okay, I love you, and by the way, will you kill my wife?" It was more like, "Ya know what, I hate her. I'm gonna kill her. I'm gonna shoot her." He kept saying that he was going to do these awful things, and I was thinking, *Okay*, like this was fine, acceptable, as if he were saying, "Pass the butter, please."

He would say, "You know what, if I get caught, I'll go to jail," and I talked about it with him, saying, "I'll tell them you were with me."

He'd respond, "You can't do that, because I'm married and you're a kid and I'm not really supposed to be with you, but I love you so much, so don't ever tell anybody."

It got to the point where he kept saying, "Oh, I'll get in all this trouble and I'll go to jail and you'll never see me again." And he'd repeat, "Will you miss me?"

"Of course I'll miss you," I told him. "I'll be devastated." I'm thinking, *I'll do this for you because I love you so much and I don't want you to get in trouble.*

He just kept leading me into it. What a damn manipulator. He would say, "Oh, you love me? You'd do that for me? You're so special. You're the greatest." So here I felt like the greatest person who ever lived because I was going to shoot somebody for someone else. How pathetic is that?

Every chance he had he would plant these thoughts in my little mind. He would say to me, "A marriage is 'till death do us part'—you just have to speed up the last part." On his boat, *Double Trouble* (what a jerk he was), he'd say, "I'd like to drive around the ocean and throw her off my boat." But then he'd complain about how long the insurance money would take to come through. And I thought all this was fine. How utterly horrible. For years I couldn't even admit that I thought it was okay. I couldn't come to terms with the fact that I could think that way.

He would obsess and daydream about getting rid of her. He'd have an argument with her and then call me, and I would tell him how wonderful he was. Here I was, a young girl building up his ego. I was just a dumb love-struck teenager who wanted to keep her boyfriend.

After I was arrested he claimed that he didn't know me and that I was a liar making all this up. But then the police began to uncover the facts—little things like him signing into hotels with me under the name Joe Berkley. Berkley, you might recall, was the name of the street I lived on.

My relationship with Joey was a series of cheap motels, good restaurants, and lies.

ABOVE:
Age 16, in spring 1991 in my backyard at home in Merrick. Hello? How many warning signs are in these photos?

LEFT:
Age 16 and headed for trouble.

ABOVE:
In my room with a lot on my mind in January 1992.

ABOVE:
Walking on the beach in Long Beach, Long Island, in April 1992, a month before all hell broke loose.

ABOVE:
One of Joey's many mug shots.

Chapter Six

THAT FATEFUL DAY

W e all come to a moment in life when one action is pivotal, when one decision becomes the catalyst that takes away years of future decisions.

May 19, 1992, is the day I replay in my mind constantly. It was the day the path I chose would alter my entire life. It was the day my actions would change the lives of so many others. It was the day I walked up to Mary Jo Buttafuoco's front door with a loaded gun.

How could I have fallen so far? Simple: I was a selective "people pleaser," and Joey was the person I wanted to please. Add being easily manipulated, living with physical and mental abuse, emotional instability, low self-esteem, and being egged on by a scheming adult, and combine that with the normal teen neuroses and lack of life experience and maturity, and you have the recipe for a disaster.

The one question people always asked me is why I shot Mary Jo. Was I crazed with jealousy? Did Joey force me to do it? They would continue prodding, insisting on a clear-cut answer. The truth was, I didn't have a good answer. Imagine not having a good reason for shooting someone!

The best I could come up with is that I wanted Joey Buttafuoco to think I was cool. I wanted his approval. It's frightening to do something like what I did and not have a concrete reason. For a long time I couldn't figure out what that reason was, but after years of self-reflection and healing, I came to the conclusion that it was because it was what Joey wanted me to do. And I did what he wanted me to do. Joey had everything to gain. I had everything to lose.

He was forever complaining about his wife.

"I hate her," he would say. "I wish she was dead."

"I sit up at night thinking of ways to kill her and get away with it," he would tell me.

As a teenager, I wasn't able to think outside the box. If Joey said she was awful, that she screamed all the time and was a horrible mother, well, to me, it had to be true. Forget that Joey had a drug problem, stayed out late at night, and cheated on her. My peers acted like that, so in my young mind those behaviors that Joey exhibited were part of the norm. It never dawned on me that he, a married man in his mid-thirties with two small children, was the one with problems. He should have been home with his family spending his money on them, not on girlfriends and drugs.

Today I can only imagine what Mary Jo's life with Joey was really like. Twelve years ago, though, I lacked the wisdom and experience that comes with age. She was a bad person just because Joey, who had so much influence over me, said so. It never even entered my mind that he could have possibly been a spoiled, overgrown child. Perhaps that's why he appealed to me in the first place. Because I was, at times, a spoiled child myself and I could identify with him.

In my mind, that disastrous spring day in 1992 has dwindled over the years to a series of momentary flashbacks. I remember parts of my life at that time, but not my life in its entirety.

It started with a request. I asked a friend of a friend for a gun. I then told Joey I was getting the gun. I said I'd shoot his wife if he wanted, so he could be free. I remember him asking to see the gun. I didn't have it yet.

"This guy Peter has it," I replied. Peter was just holding it for me.

Joey said, "No, you don't have a gun. You can't get a gun." He was amused; I was serious.

He told me, "Well, if you are going to shoot her, make sure I'm at work."

Looking back, I realize that he may not have even believed it when the police told him what had happened to Mary Jo. At the time I really believed he wanted me to shoot her.

Joey Buttafuoco was a BS artist. He toyed with me for his own pleasure. He told me outrageous stories of mob involvement that were impressive to an adolescent and that showed me he didn't play by society's rules. To me this was awesome; Joey was my idol, and I wanted to be just like him.

I knew it was wrong to shoot somebody. My parents had taught me all about right and wrong. I just didn't understand the consequences and the ramifications of doing something like that, especially when I had an adult telling me it was okay. If I had been sitting there with my teenage girlfriends and somebody suggested, "Let's shoot somebody," I would have said, "What, are you crazy?"

I didn't listen to my friends. When they used to say, "Somebody has pot, you wanna try it?" I would respond, "Are you kidding? No, I don't want to try it!" I never tried drugs because to me it was against the law and just stupid. I didn't listen to other teenagers, but I did listen to adults.

I tell you all this about Joey just so that you know the background, the influences surrounding me, and my state of mind. Now, with the clarity of time and sanity, I think he might have thought I was kidding. But that might be me—still, after all these years, under his influence—once again making excuses for him. If he really didn't want me to do it, he would have sat me down and told me it was wrong, instead of continuing to encourage me. I would have listened to him.

The bottom line, though, is that I was the one who committed the crime.

Tuesday, May 19, was beautiful—one of the nicest days of the year. Sunny and breezy … a day that was perfect for my planned trip with my friends to the Great Adventure theme park in New Jersey.

A beautiful day for sure, but a violent storm was brewing around me.

I was probably clinically insane that day. The whole morning seemed surreal. It was an out-of-body experience—straight out of a movie.

So many lives changed for the worse around 11:48 that beautiful summer-like Tuesday morning at 1 Adam Road West in Massapequa, Long Island.

I left school early that day because Peter, the boy who had the gun, said he'd take a ride with me to shoot Mary Jo, as if he were accompanying me to the mall.

I went to the school nurse, told her I was sick, and was excused for the remainder of the school day. I would have just cut my afternoon classes, but that would have been breaking the rules. (Like going to shoot someone isn't breaking the rules!) It just shows how disconnected I was that I wouldn't break a school rule but I was about to go shoot someone.

Although Peter said he'd be waiting outside my house, I half-expected him to not even show up. But when I pulled up to my house, he was waiting for me. We spent the ten-minute drive to Mary Jo's home bickering about who was going to shoot her. Peter talked tough; he was a thug, and I just always assumed he would do it. But when we got there, he said that he wouldn't do it and that I should just do it. I told him I couldn't. He then suggested that if I couldn't shoot her, I should talk to her.

That was a great idea, I thought. I got out of the car and walked toward Mary Jo's front door.

I rang the bell, and Mary Jo came to the door. I stared at her. It suddenly struck me that this was a living, breathing human being. Shockingly, I had never thought of her that way. Joey had always demonized her, and she was The Enemy to me. But here she was, suddenly, a real person.

I just stood there not saying a word.

She said, "Hello, who are you? Can I help you?"

I couldn't get my thoughts together. The moments of silence seemed like an eternity. I started to make up a story about how my sister was having an affair with Joey, just because I chickened out and wanted to get away from there without Mary Jo finding out who I really was. She kept asking me my name, over and over. I was panicking, thinking that Joey would be so angry if he found out. I had to get out of there. My mind was racing.

She asked me if I was the daughter of some man, as if she knew Joey was having an affair with someone else. I wasn't the only young girl he had been involved with. I was just the only one stupid enough to do his bidding.

I remember feeling angry as she dismissed me and started to walk away. She said she was going to call Joey. In a matter of seconds I was thinking, *Oh no, she can't call him. He'll be so angry at me. He'll think I'm a loser. He won't love me anymore.*

Mentally and physically, I was breaking down. I was dizzy and everything was spinning. I began to hit her on the head with the gun. Why? Well, that's always been the question. I think in my panic at that moment I just wanted to stop her from calling Joey. I was desperate.

I've realized over the course of time that I don't know exactly why I ultimately did what I did. There was no good reason, and I had nothing to gain. Even if I had a reason in my destructive mind, it would not have justified my actions. I was an out-of-control kid who had just hit rock bottom.

I left Mary Jo bleeding and screaming in front of her house. I was scared, and as usual I was thinking only about myself. I ran away. I didn't want to get in trouble. Like no one was ever going to find out I was the one who did this.

When I got back to the car, Peter made me return to the house to retrieve the gun. When I returned to the car, he was shocked. The gun was in pieces. Apparently when I hit her, the gun had exploded and fired.

Since then, I have rerun that moment over and over again in my head. I know why I went there, but it was so traumatic that to this day I don't know exactly what transpired. To this day, twelve years later, I still can't stop constantly reliving that blurry scene. I can be anywhere—

having fun with my family or friends at a party or a picnic, watching TV, or reading to my son—and I drift off thinking about it, and I have to snap out of it. Even as I remain haunted by this moment, however, I can't imagine Mary Jo's nightmares.

It turned out that it was not that easy to just go and shoot somebody.

I was frightened. Believe me, if somebody told you, "Take out a gun and shoot me right now," and said that there would be absolutely no consequences to you, I don't think you'd be able to do it. When soldiers go to war and are told to shoot somebody—told that they're allowed to do it—it's still very, very difficult. Can you imagine doing something like that?

I've spoken with people who have been through war, and they all say it was very hard to shoot another person or even hurt another person. I'm not just talking about getting angry and punching somebody in the nose, but actually doing grave harm to another person. You have to have a certain mentality to do that, and it turned out that, for all my bravado, I didn't have it.

So if the gun hadn't discharged, we probably just would have ended up fighting, and she would have called the police on me, and that would have been the end of it.

It turns out that this kid who let me use his gun had taken the weapon from his brother who worked for the New York City Transit Authority. His brother had this defective gun, so he threw it in a drawer. And then his kid brother Peter, the twenty-one-year-old mobster-wannabe, took it, thinking that he was cool. He just stole it, not knowing it was defective.

The case was later settled in civil court as an accident, and in criminal court the offense I eventually pleaded to was Reckless Assault with depraved indifference, which means I did it and instead of staying there and calling the police and doing the right thing, I left.

I take 100 percent responsibility for what I did to Mary Jo that day.

I was so scared after the incident. I remember yelling at Peter, just screaming at him, "I never want to see you again. I hate you!" and slamming the car door.

I yelled, "Don't ever call me, I hate your guts." I was blaming him, thinking, *Why did you let me do this?*

Imagine, I was blaming Peter as if I were not responsible at all. I was so immature and out of touch with reality that I thought if I never saw him again somehow it would be as though the last hour never occurred.

He eventually agreed to be a witness against me if I went to trial, which I didn't. He was prepared to say anything they wanted him to say. In exchange for that, he was in prison for about four months. In jail the Mafia wannabe probably ended up turning into a scared little boy, which I could understand. We were all terrified. We were so young.

That afternoon of the shooting I went to Nassau Community College to register for the fall semester, although I was hoping to attend the Fashion Institute of Technology in New York City. If I didn't go to register at Nassau, my parents would yell at me and I would get in trouble. I couldn't have that.

I registered, the whole time thinking of Mary Jo, what I had just done, and wishing I never did it.

I was saying to myself all day, *Please let her be okay.* I was terrified. I had spent so much time listening to Joey's mobster tales that violence had become an exciting fantasy. I had just learned that afternoon that violence is frightening.

I returned home, and I knew I would be in trouble. But I was so stupid—I thought the trouble would all be with my parents. I never even thought about the police. Remember, Joey said everything would be okay.

I recall going home and just saying, "Oh my God, oh my God, I'm so sorry. I'll never do it again. I'll be the best person ever."

I thought it was still going to go away. I kept promising, "I'm gonna be the greatest person who ever lived. I'm gonna stop world hunger. I'm gonna bring peace to the world. Just forgive me."

I believed that, since I was vowing to be a great, perfect person, all my problems would disappear.

Remember when you were young and you did something wrong, like receiving a bad report card, and you would make all sorts of pacts to get out of it? You'd say, "Dear God, I apologize. I'll never do it again. I'll get A's from now on." It was that same mentality. But I was really, really sorry. Not because I *was* really sorry, but because I was scared.

The impact of what I had done had not gotten through to me. It was still like getting a bad report card. I never thought about Mary Jo dying. I just thought that I had left her and she was hurt, and then when I turned on the news later that day and saw that she was in the hospital, I thought, *Oh, thank God she's okay.* Like being shot was the equivalent of falling off your bicycle.

After it happened, I was so frightened that I told all my friends. I was apologizing to all of them, and they were saying to me, "It's okay. Don't worry, it's okay."

While I watched the news that night, the impact of what happened began sinking in. But I, the stupid kid, thought that because of my regret there would be no more consequences. It never crossed my mind—I had no understanding — that this was against the law, that there were prisons, that I would go to one. No, I'm just going to go to school tomorrow, and it will be business as usual, because I didn't mean it.

Mary Jo was alive. I was relieved to know she would live. I wasn't worried about getting in trouble. She didn't know my name, and I knew Joey wouldn't ever tell anyone it was me (or so I thought). But I had told all my friends!

I didn't understand the enormity of what I had just done. I didn't understand that I would have to be held accountable.

The day after the shooting I went to school, studied, and did my homework. But I was thinking about the shooting. Oh my God, that's all I could think about. As if all this weren't crazy enough, I remember something snapping in my head and saying to myself, *I don't want to be with Joey anymore.* I was starting to realize that his tales of violence and his anything-goes attitude weren't as glamorous as I had thought.

Although I felt terrible about what I had done, I was still remarkably clueless. I wasn't even waiting for the cops to show up and arrest me. Joey would protect me. I still did not understand that I could or ultimately would be arrested and go to a prison.

This is all very painful for me to relive. It's difficult for me to have to admit to myself and the world that I committed such an atrocious act of violence. For years I've danced around this topic when others have brought it up. It's troubling and embarrassing. But I realized while writing this book that I had to address my own culpability. It is my hope that by doing so my past will help others out there who are currently in situations that seem beyond their control and impossible to get out of.

There are many other girls and women out there who can identify with my life, whether they have been abused or lack self-esteem or are full of themselves or don't candidly talk to their parents or others about their problems. I know they are out there because they write to me all the time. Do you recognize the girl I was, the girl I've been describing? Am I you? Your daughter? Your sister? Your mother? Your best friend? Your classmate? Your neighbor?

Take my story as a cautionary tale.

Chapter Seven

THE ARREST

After the shooting, when the police questioned Joey, he suggested that Paul Makely, a twenty-nine-year-old gym owner I was dating at the time, might have been responsible. He said that Paul had it in for him, and he mentioned Makely's girlfriend, whose name he didn't know — me.

I met Paul a few months before my arrest. Another grown-up who should have known better, he owned a gym where I exercised, and we started to date. I was seeing him and Joey. Joey knew about Paul. Joey was my father figure; Paul was my boyfriend.

Apparently Joey just happened to give the police an off-the-cuff "possible" scenario of what "might have" occurred on the doorstep that was remarkably similar to what actually transpired.

My home, my parents, and I had been under surveillance for days. On May 21, about 7:00 P.M., the police followed me as I drove away from my house. They waited about ten minutes so they could pick me up away from my home, because they wanted to take me into custody alone. They didn't want my parents or an attorney around while they interrogated me, which was illegal because I was a minor. I was pulled over in my car, and a policeman started walking toward me. Amazingly, when I first heard the sirens, I thought I was being pulled over for a traffic violation. I soon realized it was more than that. The policemen asked me to come with them. I had no idea that Joey had told the police who I was and where to find me.

Since the police wanted to get me alone, they asked Joey, who at first claimed he didn't know me (which they knew was false), to page me and arrange a time for me to meet with him.

Not only weren't my parents notified about my arrest, but the police did not even tell them that I was in custody. In fact, my parents reported me missing, and law enforcement still didn't tell them. They just took a missing person report. The police wanted me isolated. They, like so many other adults in my life, knew they could take advantage of this troubled kid.

But I was still in denial. My first thought when they arrested me was, *Oh boy, I'm in trouble now.* I was afraid my parents would find out and punish me. I never had any idea about the real consequences, so I just kept telling the police, "I don't know anything."

I was handcuffed to a chair. They didn't let me use the bathroom. After a while, when I told them I was hungry, they brought in a cheeseburger and put it on the other side of the table from me. I was also thirsty, and they brought in a Pepsi and waited until something I said was pleasing to them and then they let me drink some. It was psychological torture. They did this for hours and hours. There were hot lights shining on me. It's not just something you see in the movies. It's real. This is why there are so many false confessions. You just want the torture to stop.

Studies consistently show that torturing prisoners does not extract reliable information. Prisoners will tell you whatever you want to hear just to end the abuse.

And that's what happened with me. Finally, I said, "Okay," after hours and hours of questioning. I was agreeing to all sorts of things just to get them to leave me alone. They handed me a statement and said, "Sign this and you can go home."

And I was thinking, *I'll sign anything as long as you let me go home.*

"Okay, I did it."

And they said, "Well, we know you did it. You could have told us this seven hours ago."

But until the very end I was still protecting Joey, even though the police were showing me evidence that he had set me up.

"He's not your friend. He's not on your side," they would tell me. But at that time I thought he was, and I kept quiet about him.

Looking back at it now, after watching too many episodes of *Law & Order*, I realize they were working the good-cop-bad-cop routine. It was all a game. The seriousness of what happened was lost on me. I was a kid, and I was just terrified, and I wanted to go home.

The police were telling me, "We understand. Just tell us everything, and then we'll call your parents, and you can go home." And I said, "Oh God, you can't tell my parents. Can I just go home?"

This disconnect on my part was bizarre. I thought I'd tell the cops what happened and they wouldn't tell Mommy and Daddy. I didn't want to get punished. Forget about going to jail. It wasn't even on my mind. I didn't even understand that I *could* go to jail. I just didn't want to get punished and have my privileges taken away. Is that unbelievable? I was thinking, *They're going to take away my car and ground me.*

I couldn't tell them about Joey because I loved him, and he told me he could get in trouble, and I didn't want him to get in trouble. He had assured me that I couldn't get in trouble because of my age, so at this point I was thinking the worst trouble I could get in was that they were going to tell my parents.

I just told them what they wanted, and I figured that I was going to go home.

And I asked, "Okay, can I go home now?"

And they said, "No, you're going to jail."

I said, "What? I can't go to jail. What are you talking about?" And the next thing I knew I was put in handcuffs and thrown in a jail cell.

Thinking back on it now, I was so naïve and young. At one point I suggested to the cops that if Mary Jo would drop the charges, I would move to France.

I did not want to see my parents after I was arrested because I was afraid that I was going to be in trouble and they were going to be very disappointed. I didn't want that, so I told my lawyer, Christine Edwards Neumann, "I'm scared to see them. I don't want to see them."

She said, "Don't worry, I'll talk to them." She spoke with them and came back and said, "I talked to your parents. They love you, and they want to see you, and they're not going to yell at you." So she assured me and set me at ease.

I assumed she warned them, "You're not allowed to yell at her because she's fragile."

So they came to the jail, and my mother was crying hysterically, and my father was trying not to scream at me and strangle me.

We sat there at a table, and my mother was holding my hands and wanting to take me home. My father was just sitting there. I could tell that he just wanted to wring my neck like a chicken. He was not saying anything. And I could tell he wanted to cry, and they were just so devastated.

I was telling them, "I'm sorry." I was crying and saying, "I didn't mean it." My mother was saying, "Oh, I know you didn't mean it, dear, it's okay." She was out of touch with reality, which is understandable considering it's not every day when a mother is told that her child shot someone.

I sat there for months in this run-down jail, watching myself on TV, miraculously becoming the Long Island Lolita.

I called my mother from the jail one day to ask her, "What's a Lolita?" It was comical. I might as well have been five years old with my maturity level.

In addition to the sensational crime, one iconic photo helped fuel the fire. At 3:00 P.M. the day following my arrest, after Joey told the police that he'd like to "wring my neck" and that they should take the jailhouse key and throw it away, I was walked to the Nassau County Courthouse to be arraigned. I was wearing the cut-off shorts and white T-shirt I was arrested in, and my eggplant-tinted hair was blowing in the wind. When this picture hit the press, it set the scene for the tabloid frenzy that was to come.

It was an era just primed for a case like this. A lot of things conspired against me—not the least of which was a burgeoning, ruthless, and sleazy tabloid news media with no ethics. Everyone involved in the case got caught up in it.

I committed a crime, but they furthered the crime by exploiting an underage girl. They made such a mockery of the case that even Mary Jo, the real victim, was viewed by the public as a joke in a white-trash soap opera. And throughout it there was this man who caused it all—Joey Buttafuoco. He ate it all up, denied the truth, played to the camera, and made a fortune off the tragedy he created.

I like to think that if I had been on the outside I would have had great compassion for this young girl who was being exploited at all turns, a girl who was being dragged further and further down and not receiving any help.

In reliving this now, as I write this book, I have to tell you that it is truly amazing that I came out whole on the other side of that awful time.

Chapter Eight

IN JAIL

I n the Nassau County Jail, I was isolated. And because mine was already a high-profile case from the start, there were news cameras everywhere. I never saw anything like it. Actually there was *nothing* like it.

The case was high profile for several reasons: it involved sex, adultery, and a white, supposedly affluent teenage girl from the suburbs. If I had been from a poor minority community and lived in foster care, nobody would have cared. I would have been another sad statistic who disappeared as an obscure brief blurb on page 30 of the newspaper.

Because I was so high profile, they put me in a cell all by myself.

They also decided that since I was a teenage white girl from a nice town, I had to have committed the crime because I was mentally ill, so they put me on suicide watch. They took away my shoelaces, and I was sitting there saying to myself, *Uh-oh. Things are only going to get worse.*

I was sitting in jail on suicide watch when I first met lawyer Eric Naiburg. My original lawyer, Christine Edwards Neumann, recommended Eric, who was a dashing News 12 commentator. My parents went up to his summer home in Woodstock, New York, to meet him and hired him on the spot. He quickly became my "savior": "Don't worry, little girl, I'm gonna get you out of this horrible place."

He was very nice to me, and I was so young that I just wanted people to like, to latch onto, because I had no identity of my own.

I was in the miserable Nassau County Jail for a little more than two months—sixty-six days.

Here's a brief graphic description of Nassau County Jail: They threw you in a cell. There were no pillows. There were no blankets. There was no soap. There was no hairbrush. There were field mice scurrying around all night. There were small portions of hard-to-identify food. There were no books, and there was limited TV. They locked you in a cell for about twenty hours a day. So you just sat there all day on a bed, which was basically a metal slab covered with a piece of foam.

I had long beautiful hair. There was no way to comb it. It was turning into balls of matted hair. They finally put me in with other teenagers, most of whom were black and were locked up for minor things like shoplifting a shirt. The girls decided they were going to cornrow my hair so it wouldn't fall out. It was really nice of them, and I really appreciated it. But when I left prison, I was quite a sight with my cornrowed hair. Bo Derek I was not.

They gave you Corcraft soap in jail. It was just a bar of lye. It made me break out in big, red hives, so I couldn't wash. As disgusting as it sounds, I was just a little greaseball.

They didn't give you enough food. What they did give you was generic in order to accommodate people with health problems such as diabetes, so it contained no type of salt or seasoning. All the food was bland. You can't imagine how bad that was. So I lived on milk. I lost about twenty pounds in those two months. I just sat there with no pillows, no blankets, listening to water drip, freezing, starving, and watching the mice scamper across the floor.

I sat there and stared at the wall. That's it. At that point, I was receiving thousands of supportive letters every week, so day after day, with nothing at all else to do, I read all my "fan" mail. That was my entertainment. I didn't realize then that many viewed me as a victim of both Joey and the legal system. I was thinking to myself, *These people love me.* How pathetic. I had just shot somebody.

At the time, though, I believed that I was going to get out of there, because everything was fine now that people knew that I felt bad about what I had done.

You know what? I wasn't sorry. I was sorry in my own little juvenile, limited capacity, but I didn't understand what being truly remorseful was. To feel true remorse, you have to understand why you did what you did, and that took many, many years.

Chapter Nine

BAILED OUT

I had a $2 million bail—at the time, the largest in Nassau County history. To secure the bond for that amount of bail, my parents put their house up as collateral. That raised $1.2 million. Eric got a production company, KLM, to put up the remaining amount to secure the bond for the huge bail. In exchange, KLM received the exclusive rights to my story.

Eric sold my soul for two months of freedom. I was told it would be more time than that. He told my parents it would be forever. In retrospect, what Eric Naiburg did was horrible, and I will tell you more about it later in the book.

Eric said he would defend me so that I would never see another day of prison. My parents believed him. They signed on the dotted line thinking that, since I was a kid and "it was all Joey Buttafuoco's fault," they'd get me into rehabilitation and get me help. Eric convinced them that I would not go to prison. So they thought that they were signing to get me out of prison permanently. If they had known it was for two months, they would have never made that deal. They would have left me there but preserved my rights to my own life. They were emotionally distraught and having marital problems at the time. Eric did a number on them.

The deal was that a book was to be written, and it was. And that book would be turned into a movie, and it was. My interview with the author was at a hotel in Manhattan. I spoke with her for about an hour, and then she came to see me in prison for several hours after I was sentenced and sent to Albion Correctional Facility in upstate New York. I had been there for maybe four or five days, and the publishing house was pestering Eric at the time, saying, "We have to get in. We need to speak to her." I was just mentally not even there. I was new to this terrible environment, devastated, and here was this writer poking into my life. I was very uncooperative.

I didn't want to talk to her, but Eric kept telling me, "You have to. They'll sue you. You have to cooperate."

I had very little input into that book, by my own choosing. I was difficult and didn't want to participate. Although it was a sympathetic read and the author, Sheila Weller, was an excellent writer, most of the facts came from Weller's interviews with others and not from me. It was Eric who provided most of the detail. I call it Eric's book. It really was not my story, even though it was called that.

This is how it really went: In the book, Weller talks about our time together as four days, filled with insightful bonding. The truth is the time I spent with her could be counted in hours. I only met with her twice. The first time was in the Westbury Hotel, in New York City. Eric brought me there and we argued the whole way because I didn't want to tell my life story. He made me comply. We got to the hotel suite about 5 P.M. (Eric had to work that day so we drove into the city late.) I had one bedroom, which was connected to a living room area, and on the other side of that was another bedroom, Weller's. I sat in a chair, Eric in another chair, and Weller in a third. It was like going to a psychologist for the first time. I didn't want to be there and talk was awkward. I didn't really want to share myself with her. We chitchatted for an hour or so, moving from pleasantries to Joey in ten minutes.

I finally had enough of the grilling and declared I was hungry. We got up and I told Eric I didn't like her, she just rubbed me the wrong way. We didn't click. I told him I did not want to sit through a dinner with her.

Eric spoke to Weller privately and I went to one of the bedrooms. I watched Bill and Hillary Clinton; it was election night 1992.

Eric and I went to dinner. I begged him not to leave me alone that night but he told me I had to speak with her. By the time we got back to the hotel it was late. I said I was tired and went to my room. I got on the phone with friends. The next morning I spoke to Weller briefly while we were dressing to leave. I was told I had to meet with her associates for a quick breakfast, and I begrudgingly went. Soon after, a car picked me up at the restaurant and brought me back to Long Island. Later I learned from my friends that Weller got the phone log from the hotel with my friends' phone numbers and called everyone on the list (what nerve) to question them for the book. No one knew who she was or what to say. When I found out, I went from finding this to be an annoyance to absolutely hating her. More than ever I wanted nothing to do with her or the book. I refused to ever see her again.

Toward the end of December, after I was in Albion a few days, I spoke with Eric and he told me Weller was coming to talk to me and he told me I had to be nice. I complied, but how could I open up to someone I didn't trust, someone I felt had just violated me? I didn't tell her much. I wanted to make her job hard. That was it, a few hours in an Albion's visiting room. I never saw her again. But the book was filled with incidents, details, quotes, and intimate feelings of mine that were pure fiction.

In 1992, during one of the lowest points of my chaotic life, I was unable to look back at that life in any reflective or objective manner. To think that I could write a book at that time, or even to contribute to one in a productive or reflective manner, was a ridiculous concept. It took many years for me to mature and heal enough to be able to look back on my life with a worthwhile and insightful perspective.

The money from that book went toward production people and writers. People think I got rich off that book. I never saw a dime.

I wanted to get out of jail. I couldn't think rationally about signing that deal. I was a screwed-up, stressed-out kid. "Just get me out of here," I kept saying. And here was Eric telling me, "I'm selling your rights. It will help get you out of there." What did I know?

Had I been in a different state of mind and fully aware of what I was doing, I absolutely, definitely, would not have agreed to that arrangement. I was completely ignorant of my rights. I had no understanding of "notoriety" or even of how to gain control over my own life story. At that point I was just a teenager who could not even control when I could eat, wash my hair, or even decide what soap to use. That book wouldn't have had to be written, and that movie, based on the book (the movie shown on NBC, starring Noelle Parker), would never have come to fruition.

I also had to participate in interviews with programs like *Dateline*. In fact, there were a couple of interviews that KLM made me do from the prison. If you view those interviews now you will see that I was very unhealthy, both mentally and physically. I was still being exploited at every turn. And I was powerless.

Eric sold my soul to the devil, and my frightened, naïve parents signed on the dotted line. It was horrendous.

In retrospect, I don't think Eric ever did anything good for me. He was a terrible choice of attorney for me. Oh yes, he did do something good. He brought me to some great restaurants. That's about it. He was a nice guy. I can't say he wasn't that. He was very charming, very likable, and we became very close. Too close. But in the long run he didn't do anything positive for me legally. He didn't do what he was hired to do. His inappropriate behavior and deceptions are what eventually helped get me out of jail. Like so many others involved in the case, he got caught up in the media frenzy. More about Eric later.

What I needed was an attorney more concerned with taking care of my legal problems than with getting movie deals for me and TV interviews for himself. If I had had a different attorney, I think I would have been much better off. I would have done better with the legal system, and I would have turned into a better person much sooner.

First of all, if I'd had an attorney who was looking out for my best interest, he would have gotten me out on bail and would have made sure I had psychiatric attention. He would not have let my parents let me run wild out of the house. He would have addressed the issues.

When I finally did get out on bail on Tuesday, July 28, 1992, I just went home, took a shower, and went out to dinner with my parents, Eric, and his defense team. We had a great meal. A victory meal. It took a while before my family and I realized that it was a victory dinner for Eric, not for us.

After the dinner it was business as usual. I was hanging out with my friends, hanging out with boys, getting into more trouble. Even at that point, nobody— not my parents or anyone else—put any limits on me.

And then there was my eighteenth birthday party. My whole family was there. Everybody was bringing me gifts, buying me things like jeans for the next year. I think back and have to laugh: "Hello? I'm going to jail. You're all adults, don't you realize this?" No, let's just throw her a big birthday party and be in denial. They were all in denial. Everybody was in denial. Eric Naiburg was going to be my savior, and since I was just a kid he was going to get me off.

No one was there to say to me: "You cannot shoot somebody and then apologize and all is forgiven. It doesn't work like that." But I think they loved me so much that they weren't thinking clearly. Also, it turns out that Eric had told them that I would not be returning to prison, so I guess it was a kind of celebration for them.

When I was out on bail, I remember being in my bedroom and hearing my parents yelling, so I came out of my room to listen. We had a large house, and I remember standing at the top of the staircase, eavesdropping on them down below me. My father was screaming at my mother because my mother just wasn't getting it. She was saying that she loved me and she was going to get me help, and then, "We're going to be a happy family again and put it all behind us." And he was screaming at her, "What, are you crazy? She ruined our whole lives. She's going to prison. She's gonna have to live with this forever. Look at these cameras outside our house. Do you understand what's going on?"

And I was standing there thinking about my father: *You're such an asshole. I didn't ruin my life.* I wanted to believe what my mother was saying. I didn't want to deal with reality, so I was angry with my father, thinking, *Ugh, I hate him, he's such an asshole.*

But in reality, he was right. He wanted to get me help, and he was just totally helpless, because my mother, my relatives, my attorney, in fact everyone, ignored the need to get me any type of psychological counseling. Everyone was focused on blaming Joey. They all agreed that if it weren't for him, none of this would be happening.

When my father realized that I was listening at the top of the stairs, he tried to tell me, "Don't you understand what you did? You ruined your whole life." And I just went back to my room, slammed my door in his face, and locked my door.

My behavior didn't change when I was out on bail. I was still the same confused teen who needed a lot of help. I was still finding all the wrong guys.

Joey might have been leading me on, but what I had been looking for at the time I was dating him was a surrogate father. Not only was Joey that surrogate father, but he was able to manipulate my real father. I always wanted that *Father Knows Best* kind of dad, but I didn't have it with my father, nor did I have it with Joey. But it wasn't just a father figure I was seeking at the time. I was also looking for a boyfriend.

Paul Makely was twenty-nine when I met him, not married, attractive, and he was more what I was looking for in terms of boyfriend material. It's strange, but I wasn't madly in love with Joey. I thought I loved him, but it was more like I ran to him for comfort, for advice, to have an adult male to really talk deeply to when I needed to. Paul was superficial fun.

He and I went out for about two months. To a teenager, dating for two months is a long time. Paul was someone who filled a temporary void for me. I knew little about him except that he had muscles, a boat, and a Corvette. To the juvenile mind, these things mean fun, fun, fun—and that we had, on a superficial level. I never really talked to him much about myself. I didn't really like myself at that point, so what would I tell him?

When I was arrested, I called Paul from Nassau County Jail. I told him I had been arrested, but he thought I was kidding. I told him I wasn't. I then began to tell him what I had done. I thought he'd be horrified, but he wasn't. It was like what I did was just part of day-to-day life. He told me something to the effect of, "Get out soon, so we can hang out." I was so relieved that he wasn't angry. It never dawned on me that he wasn't angry because I was just some dime-a-dozen girl he was messing around with who meant nothing. Just like I was with Joey. There were plenty more where I came from. I guess for them it was, "Okay, next in line."

The day after I was released on bail, I was annoyed about all the news trucks parked in front of my house, but otherwise it was life as usual. The seriousness of my actions had not caught up with me yet. My attorneys advised my parents not to upset me—it would only make things worse. Worse? A good kick in the butt was long past due and probably was just what was needed at the time. But there were no rules, not even in this serious time of crisis. I grabbed my car keys and came and went as I pleased. The Joey thing didn't work out, so it was like, oh well, Paul is still around. So as Mary Jo lay seriously injured, I spent the summer at the beach and waterskiing off Paul Makely's boat. Life was all about me, and I had no one around me telling me otherwise.

I thought Paul was my friend. It never dawned on me that he was still hanging around me because he was savvy enough to realize my story was worth a great deal of money and just maybe he could be a beneficiary. In late August 1992, I turned eighteen. Paul didn't even give me a birthday card, one of the many indications that I ignored that I meant little or nothing to him. The following week I saw Paul for the last time.

He was finally given an opportunity to cash in on his commodity: me. For $50,000, he agreed to let the sleazy tabloid television show *Hard Copy* install a video camera in his place of business. The show gave him a list of questions they wanted him to ask me and rehearsed the script with him, even telling him where he should guide me to stand so the camera could get the best view of me. Unaware, I sat behind the cash counter waiting for Paul to close up shop and watched as he counted out the register and balanced his books. He smoothly made what I thought was idle chitchat and was asking me a bunch of ridiculous hypothetical questions. Questions like, "If you could be anywhere but here right now, where would it be and what would you be doing?" We had never had such a heavy-duty, deep conversation like this before. He was so persistent with some questions that I actually became annoyed with him.

The most insistent question—the one I'll never forget—was: "For all your pain and suffering, if you could have any car in the whole world, what would it be?" I thought it was a stupid question, and after avoiding it for several minutes, I finally answered, "For all my pain and suffering, I want a red Ferrari." If you didn't see it aired, you can just imagine how bad that sounded.

Hard Copy created a script for him, Paul would ask me a question, and they'd air the answer to a different question. Or he'd ask me a question like the car one that would sound incriminating when it was taken out of context. They manipulated it to make me sound like a heartless maniac. The list of hypothetical questions he asked me went on for a while, giving *Hard Copy* a lot of material to choose from.

Several nights later, on September 24, *Hard Copy* aired the segment. The show was explosive. It was an unethical travesty designed to boost ratings. And that it did.

At the time we didn't sue them to play the real, uncut version. I didn't know anything about these sorts of things, and nobody else on my end did anything to correct it. All I was doing after it aired was crying and feeling like I wanted to die.

One thing I did know was that what was aired wasn't the way it all happened. *Hard Copy* wrote the script and knew exactly what they were going to do with it. They had it worked out before they even gave it to Paul. He just performed his part in the "play" for $50,000. (Years later, while I was still in prison, *Hard Copy*, under new management and wanting an interview, contacted me and apologized for the hatchet job they admitted they'd done in misrepresenting me. "We don't do that anymore," they told me. It was a little late for their apology—the damage had been done.)

When the segment ran on TV, it was exactly the moment when I realized I could not trust anybody. People were deceiving me left and right. They couldn't wait to make money off of me.

Another truly bad thing about this *Hard Copy* segment was that after it aired Prosecutor Klein called a press conference to announce that the authorities would stop pursuing a case against Joey and his participation in the shooting, since my credibility as a witness was now zero.

Paul wrote to me when I was in prison. He told me he was thinking about me and he missed me and he said how important I was in his life.

Did he really think I was going to write back to him after he betrayed me like that? He probably needed money again. He could then publish the "Amy Fisher Jail Letters."

People did sell fake letters, though. Throughout this whole time they sold fake items and fake letters to the tabloids.

There was nothing I could do about that, because at the time I was isolated in prison and powerless. When you're a kid and you're sitting behind bars all by yourself, you don't have anybody to help you. The media will trample you without regard to how it might affect you or your constitutional rights. They don't care because they know you're not going to do anything. If they do it once and test the waters and realize, "Hey, she didn't sue, she didn't do anything," they get bolder with each time. They get to the point where it's out-and-out lies and they realize their target is not going to do anything to remedy it. More bad advice from Eric: "Child, we can't fight them. It's not in your best interest."

Now you may understand one of the reasons why I wanted to become a journalist. People ask me why I want to get into the public eye again when I attempted for so long to stay out of it. I realized it would give *me* a chance to do the reporting—but fair and square, balanced and truthful—the way the news is supposed to be reported. I could right some wrongs. I could be an advocate for those who can't speak up for themselves. I could express myself for the first time in over a decade.

I had never given much thought to how notoriety changes someone's life. I recall seeing the infamous videotape of "Preppie Murderer" Robert Chambers in which he seemingly pretends to rip the head off a doll; the interpretation was that the doll represented his victim, Jennifer Levin.

At the time I was disgusted. I thought, *How awful. How can he make a joke like that after what happened?* It wasn't until I was thrust into that same infamous spotlight that I realized that things aren't always as they appear on TV. He too could have been set up, and the video could very well have been edited and taken out of context, as mine was.

Eric finally determined that I should see a psychiatrist. He realized that I was depressed. What a genius! The psychiatrist gave me antidepressant medicine. So what does a depressed person do? They swallow all the pills. I was so distraught by what *Hard Copy* and Makely had done to me that I tried to kill myself.

It was a culmination of doing what I did to Mary Jo, being arrested, being in jail, coming home, losing friends, and having friends who betrayed me. It was the final straw for me in my pathetic life—a life in which I had done something so horrible to another human being. I felt like I had no one, and every guy I dated told me what I wanted to hear and then turned on me. *Hard Copy* was the catalyst. The whole world thought I was a monster. I knew I wasn't, but if the world thought I was so horrible, maybe I shouldn't be here anymore.

I took the whole bottle of pills. My mother found me. She came up to my room and I was slipping into unconsciousness. So did she call an ambulance? No. She called Naiburg. She waited for him to come all the way to Nassau County from Suffolk County and then drive me back to Suffolk County to Huntington Hospital. He didn't take me any place local; instead, he took me to Huntington, forty-five minutes away, because he knew where it was. When I got there, they pumped my stomach and locked me up in the psych ward for a month.

I don't think I actually wanted to die. I wanted somebody to help me and feel sorry for me, I guess.

Eric asked Makely why he had betrayed me. Makely's response: Well, for the money. He swore the television show had lied to him, telling him they only wanted to get a glimpse into my day-to-day life. He claimed they were so nice and told him they felt bad for me and would show a sweet segment portraying my "human" side. He said he figured he would get some money and help my image at the same time. By the time he wrote those few letters to me in prison, his apologies meant nothing to me. He wasn't sorry enough to give back the $50,000 he was paid, and I wasn't about to write back to give him the opportunity to make $50,000 more off of my troubles.

When I was released from the hospital, I stayed home for only a week, and then I returned to jail. Eric felt that I should start my time early—to keep me out of trouble—so he called the prosecutor, Fred Klein, and arranged for my return. Eric came to my house to get me and literally dragged me out of there. He threw me over his shoulder, and we fell down the stairs. I didn't know what was going on, and they brought me to the courthouse against my will. Eric said he was trying to help me. I did plead guilty, but I had expected to stay out on bail at least until my sentencing hearing.

All of this bad news for me was more good news for Joey. Besides the thought that there was so much negative attention on me that there would be no way prosecutors could use my now-tainted testimony to help bolster their case against him, they were also following Mary Jo's request not to pursue her husband, who she continued to devotedly support.

You can't pick and choose whom you're going to arrest. If you're guilty, you're guilty. They didn't arrest him until he finally annoyed them more and more with his arrogant TV and radio appearances and continued brazen lies. The police, and then the prosecutors, eventually went after him. It only took six months! Finally they were ready to make him pay for his actions and, in doing so, vindicate me. Too bad I didn't feel vindicated.

ABOVE: My parents, Rose and Elliot, at a celebration dinner after I had just been released on bail in July 1992.

Chapter Ten

RETURN TO COUNTY JAIL

fter two months of freedom (plus one month in the psych ward), I returned to Nassau County Jail. It was just a nightmare, because when I had gotten out on bail, I'd thought, *I'm free. I'll never go back. It's over. Eric Naiburg told me he's going to save me.*

But instead, I ended up returning to that rat-hole county jail for two weeks before being transferred to an upstate prison to serve out the five- to fifteen-year sentence I had received. (I would spend several days at Bedford Hills Correctional Facility, in Westchester, a northern suburb of Manhattan, and then seven years upstate in the brutal Albion Correctional Facility, twenty minutes from Canada. There were three months toward the end of 1993 when I returned to Bedford Hills to prepare for Joey's Statutory Rape sentencing.)

In Nassau, the conditions were horrendous, but the guards were fine. They were regular working people. They were not abusive or nasty. For the most part, they were nice to me and did their jobs, unlike what I would later encounter in Albion.

There I was, back in county jail, in the little windowless, airless cell. I went in there with the clothes on my back, and I wore the same pair of underwear every day.

Your family is allowed to provide you with clothes, but you have to wait two weeks until you can get anything from the outside world, and I had already been moved to Bedford Hills by that time.

But even the first time I was at Nassau County Jail they gave my mother a really hard time. They'd make her wait on a line for three hours to bring me something, and then they'd tell her, "She can't have this, it's the wrong color." Or, "She's not allowed to have this brand," and they'd throw it back at her.

What they told her was totally untrue. I would inform my mother about the exact items the other women in there had, and I asked her to get the same thing. But because I was high profile and I was on TV, many jail employees were mean to me, and they were very mean to my mother. She would stand on line for three hours, and she would leave in tears because they would just throw all the stuff back at her, and she knew that I was sitting in there with no underwear and no hairbrush, nothing. As a mother, knowing that and seeing me in such lousy conditions, she was devastated and often hysterical. I'd hear from my aunts about the state she was in, upset and crying. It was just awful.

As I sat in the county jail, a reality sank in: *I'm going to be in prison for two years.* That's what Eric kept telling me: "You go there for two years and some change. It will go fast."

There I was, in county jail waiting to be transferred to prison, and Eric was coming to visit me every single day. He brought me all my press clippings. Basically, I was a movie star to him. I was sitting there in prison greens with no hairbrush, begging for a bar of Dove soap, and he was all enamored with Amy Fisher the Celebrity, his star client.

Back then, though, I did not realize this.

He would sit there and say, "You'll get out. You'll make movies."

He really had a very similar mentality to Joey about exploiting the notoriety of this case, saying, "There's all this attention, there's millions to be made. You'll go into movies, you're pretty." And I was sitting there saying, "Okay, that sounds better than this." Fixated with the media attention, Eric loved being seen with Amy Fisher — it was a thrill for him. It was very strange. He was just another guy I was following. I just wanted somebody to like me, to care about me. I was so screwed up.

I was also becoming really angry, because here I was in jail and Joey was running around, lying through his teeth, on all these TV shows.

When I was first arrested, the tabloid TV show *A Current Affair* paid him and Mary Jo half a million dollars for an exclusive interview in which Joey sat there and said about me: "She's crazy. I never had an affair with her. She's where she belongs." And I was thinking, *That bastard, just a month ago he was saying, 'I love you, you're the best thing that ever happened to me.' Now you're getting half a million dollars, holding your wife's hand, saying you love her so much, and* I'm *nuts?*

I was very angry. It went from extreme love to extreme hatred very quickly — it's said there is a fine line between the two. I hated him because it began to dawn on me what he had done to me. I realized he had scammed me, and I realized exactly what was going on. I was thinking, *Oh my God, here I am now. I'm the crazy kid and nobody believes me.* And that stigma followed me through seven years.

Joey was running free, and I was off to prison. The deal Eric told us he had worked out with the DA's office was that I would plead guilty to Reckless Assault One for a five- to fifteen-year sentence, and that I would only be in prison for two years and nine months, and then I'd be out on a work-release program.

This turned out to be completely false. He also told my parents that I would be at Bedford Hills for my entire sentence and that Bedford Hills was like a country club. Because of its proximity, he said, my mother could easily visit. But that was also completely untrue. The reality is that the minute your sentence hits the five-year mark, they transfer you upstate to Albion. He either lied or never inquired as to where I would be sent.

I just wanted to get my time over and done with. So when they brought me to Bedford Hills to begin serving out those two years and nine months, I was prepared.

There I was, eighteen years old, in a little van, on my way to Bedford Hills, a real prison.

Chapter Eleven

TABLOID '90s

At the start, it really wasn't so much my prison living circumstances I couldn't handle as the media attention. That was a lot for a teenager to deal with.

I didn't like it at all. That's why I didn't get out of prison and pursue all the things I was offered, like movies or *Playboy* or media interviews. I just tried to lay low. It's not so much fun when you go to Dairy Barn to buy a quart of milk and the paparazzi are behind you.

When I was released from prison, I was followed regularly for two years. (I am still followed, but not as constantly as before.) I used to always move. I would eventually be found and followed again. My family's residences were constantly being staked out, and photographers and reporters would hide in front of my grandmother's house and my mother's house. It was crazy.

I have wondered for years why I was so interesting to the media. I was a nobody teenager from Long Island who shot her boyfriend's wife. That doesn't happen every day, but it does happen once in a while. I was in prison with many of the other ones you never heard of.

I've been told I was newsworthy mainly because my parents were well off and I was white. It was the first time I ever thought about wealth or race in this context. Those two aspects of my life meant to many that I "should have known better." How dare I be given luxuries that most people can only dream of, and then throw them all away? I deserved to rot in prison just for being spoiled and promiscuous. How dare I think the rules didn't apply to me, that I was better than everyone else, and that I could do whatever I pleased? This is the black-and-white version, but life has many shades.

The reality is that I didn't think I was any of these things. I never did much thinking, period. Perhaps that was the biggest reason for my downfall.

People saw me as this rich, spoiled high school kid. Before me, the media had had a field day with other young "privileged" criminals — Martin Tankleff, a Long Island teen who was convicted of killing his parents, and Robert Chambers, "the Preppie Killer." But that was the late '80s. The tabloid shows didn't exist, even though those two received some notoriety. But their lives weren't blown up as mine was. Their stories were covered on *American Justice*, in a few television biographies, and on local news programming. They didn't garner the international attention that my case received. (Just a note, by the way: Martin Tankleff's "open-and-shut case" by the Suffolk County police is currently being reviewed and is under scrutiny for being seriously flawed.)

For those of you who don't remember the times, you have to understand the hoopla that surrounded this era. It was the Tabloid '90s. There was Geraldo, *A Current Affair*, *Inside Edition*, and the aforementioned *Hard Copy*.

Hard Copy started as a benign entertainment show in 1989, but it turned sleazy real quickly. The TV website jumptheshark.com best described *Hard Copy's* coverage of me: "Total sleaze…They did an entire month, twenty shows in a row, that consisted of NOTHING but bullshit, hype, speculation, screaming, and more bullshit about the 'Long Island Lolita.' Take it away."

What these shows were all about was taking the *National Enquirer* and putting it on television. And they latched onto my story. One thing would spin out of control, and then it was on to the next thing.

They would actually walk around at my high school in Bellmore and offer kids $50 to say something bad about me. People who had never even met me, who didn't know I existed until I was arrested and on TV, took the money and talked.

I remember there was one kid who went on one of those tabloid shows and said, "Oh yeah, Amy Fisher. She was gonna attack their children too, with a hacksaw." I was out on bail at the time, sitting in the living room watching TV with my parents, and this idiot kid was saying how I was going to cut kids with a hacksaw. How could I defend myself against such lies?

I was watching all these shows because at the time Eric said he wanted us to see what they were saying so I could defend myself later on. In retrospect, I think he just wanted to watch himself on TV.

It was so embarrassing watching these shows with my parents, who would get very angry because they knew I wasn't thinking about cutting people up with a hacksaw.

Or at least they didn't think so! But then again, I doubt they thought I would have done a lot of things that I in fact did.

However, the producers gave this hacksaw kid some money, and he got to be on TV. It just escalated.

And there was the wounded victim, Mary Jo, telling the press, "I love my husband. He was never with Amy." How could you not have sympathy for her and not believe her? And then Joey was walking around telling everyone who would listen, "I love Mary Jo. I don't know Amy Fisher. She's crazy."

But you know what? The more he denied our relationship—first he denied knowing me, and then he at least admitted that he knew me—and the more he said I was crazy and he never had an affair with me, the angrier I got. And from what I know now, the angrier the police and the public got.

Here you have Joey saying, "I love my wife, I never had an affair," and her saying, "I love my husband, I know he wouldn't do this," and society saying, "Bull, Joey is guilty." It became a comedy show, and everybody wanted to tune in to find out what was going to happen next.

The media used to sit outside my house, but I didn't say anything. I never talked to them. And in retrospect, I think I had bad advice.

Naiburg kept saying, "Let them say whatever they want. Don't say anything. You're above that. You're better than that." But when people say that you're "gonna cut up children with hacksaws" and you're not out there, defending the truth, saying, "You're a liar, this is crazy," the public tends to believe whoever is talking. They had to be wondering why I wasn't defending myself. It had to be true.

That's the problem I ran into. By not defending myself, I let the media have a field day with me and my image. They realized they could say anything they wanted about this young girl, and nobody was going to contradict anything—so let's run wild. And boy, did they have a good time.

That's part of why I'm writing this book now—to finally set things straight and say to the media that they can't play loose with the facts and they can't say whatever they want regardless of the truth.

I've dealt with the things that I've done. I've gone on to accept what I did and conquer my past and, I believe, become a better person. But I'm not going to deal with people making up stories, and I am just not going to put up with the lies that are still told about me from that time. What I did was bad enough. Don't compound it.

In the '90s, it was a real media circus. Whenever they'd bring me in and out for court appearances, the press was all over the place. It was like today when they escort Michael Jackson in and out of court. They had to think of alternative routes and whip out their maps. And I was thinking, *How ridiculous, just let me walk.*

They had me handcuffed and shackled, and they felt they needed to bring me through back doors, and the whole time I felt like saying, *Where do you think I'm going? Do you think I'm going to escape?* They had me shackled down like I was Jeffrey Dahmer. Where was I going to go? The NBC guy would tackle me before I got to the back door. Who were they kidding? Did they think I was going to run off to go have a bagel? As I said before, it was a comedy show, but a bad one.

Unless you witnessed it in person, there is no way to imagine the crush of the crowds, the procession of onlookers, the police officers, court officers, and press surrounding me. You would have thought that they were walking the Queen of England through the corridor.

Chapter Twelve

PRISON LIFE

To transfer me from Nassau County Jail to Bedford Hills Correctional Facility, the first thing they did was handcuff me and attach a chain to the handcuffs and wrap it three times around my waist. Then they attached me to the leg shackles like Sean Penn in the film *Dead Man Walking*. You can't actually walk when you're chained up like that. You take these half-inch steps. So the correction officers basically almost carried me to the van because it was taking me so long to get there on my own.

For a change, there were no cameras, because I was transferred in the garage of the Nassau County Jail. The press didn't even know what day I was leaving. What a relief.

I vividly recall the trip to Bedford Hills. After they shackled me and put me in the van like a wrapped-up mummy, I remember the guards opening up the window a crack in the back of the van. I was sitting there with a woman who was very quiet and didn't say too much. I was feeling air on my face for the first time in almost three weeks and looking at everything that was passing by me — tree-lined side streets, cars passing by with families in them, and people just walking around living their lives — and I was thinking how wonderful it all was.

You don't realize until you're locked in a tiny little room how much you take people walking down a landscaped street or the sound of a car horn beeping for granted. You don't realize the environment you live in, how precious it is. And I sat there thinking, *This is so nice.*

I then looked down at myself all shackled, handcuffed, disheveled, and smelly — just sitting there so degraded. I might as well have been a homeless person who was abducted. I rode all the way up to Westchester in silence just looking around at all this freedom passing me by and saying to myself, *This is it. This is gone for the next few years.*

That's when I thought it would be for only a little over two years. If I had known it would end up being seven years, who knows what I would have been thinking.

Had I known that seven years would be the outcome, I would have gone to trial. I think that if I had had the chance to tell an impartial jury my story, I would not have served as much time as I did.

Bedford Hills is in upscale Scarsdale, in New York's wealthy Westchester County. It's actually a very nice place to have a prison — million-dollar homes and Bedford Hills Correctional Facility. It seemed so out of place.

When we arrived there, I had to go through "processing:" You are on an assembly line with about 100 other women from different jails. You completely strip, the guards hose you down, they give you a bar of lye soap and put a bit of horrible-smelling disinfectant shampoo in your hair and pubic hair to kill lice and bugs, and they stand there and watch you through the whole process to make sure you do everything. After you're hosed down and disinfected they give you a thin, yellow cloth robe (since they don't provide a towel at this point the wet robe becomes see-through) and you get back on the assembly line.

You then walk past a line of tables with different clothing items on them, and as you walk down the line they determine your size (only small, medium, or large) and hand you the item—shoes, socks, pants, shirts, sweatshirt, towel, underwear, and a bra.

And then you're ready to begin your prison stay.

Bedford Hills Prison is a series of old buildings, like an old apartment complex, so immediately from the outset I saw that it was far different from the Nassau County Jail.

I expected Bedford Hills Prison to be like the jail I had just come from, where you're in a little tiny cell where you don't see the light of day. Once I realized that there was a fence around this new place, with acres and acres of property, and that you could walk around and see grass and people, it was actually a relief.

We were taken to get something to eat, and the food was decent. You go through cafeteria style. I ate a sandwich, which was great because I had not had anything substantial, except milk and cereal, for almost three weeks.

From our building I was able to see a highway and people coming and going. Free people a block away. I can't even explain that feeling.

I felt so isolated.

The strangest things become important. We take basic things for granted — like showers, food, warmth — and when those basic needs are taken away and then given back to you, it's all you think about: *Ahh, I finally had a hot shower.*

A real shower. In county jail it was just this little droplet that drips out, no shampoo, and just that bar of lye soap that you can't even use. But in Bedford I was finally given real soap and shampoo and a hot shower and some food, as well as underwear and socks. They provided inmates with a pillow and pillowcase. Here, it seemed, a prisoner's physical needs were actually taken care of.

That's all I wanted to do — go through processing and sleep for days. Sleep and eat. All I was thinking about was that I could eat and wash up. People do not usually think about those things. You wake up in the morning, you have your breakfast, you take a shower, and you don't give it a second thought. Before jail, I never did either.

Since I was all over the media, people assumed I was a high-level criminal with a maximum-security sentence. But to the Department of Corrections I was just a little peon with what they considered a minor assault charge. Although I was a medium-security prisoner, I was in maximum-security Bedford Hills.

After the food and shower, I was walked to the back of the prison into this little area with cots. It kind of looked like a homeless shelter. There was very little security. The cots were all lined up next to each other, and you could see a common area. It looked something like an old-folks home with the inmates playing cards and bingo and watching cable TV.

And they were cooking! On hot plates! Ramen noodles and Spam in a can were the big dishes there. (Ramen noodles fried in oil, not boiled, was the big treat in prison.) After my county jail experience, I thought, *This is very bizarre. What have I entered?* They even had telephones.

And then I saw men—tough-looking guys with beards, muscles, and tattoos.

With the pay phones they had there you could only call collect. I immediately went to call my mother to tell her that I was alive and that they gave me a shower and underwear and oatmeal, just so she would be relieved, because she was very worried about me. And I asked her, "Did you know this place is co-ed? There are men here."

She freaked out, saying "What?! There are men in there!? They could be rapists!" We hung up, and she immediately called the prison. She wanted to know why they had put her teenage daughter in with these guys.

She complained to the officials, "My daughter said these are mean-looking guys who have mustaches, beards, tattoos, and big muscles living with her," and they finally figured out on the other end that, no, these were women with hormone problems, lesbians they referred to as "dyke aggressors." These were women, not men.

That was my introduction to prison.

Remember how young and relatively sheltered I was. I had never encountered anything like this before. I was very confused because I was going to be living with them and they looked like men, sounded like men, and I thought they were men. So my mother had to explain to me the prison dynamics, that these were not men. She told me, "Honey, now you stay away from them if they make you uncomfortable."

That was my first prison lesson—it is not co-ed.

In both Bedford and later Albion, I would go in the bathrooms and I'd see these women who looked like men kissing women who looked like women, and they were doing sexual things in the toilet stalls when I'd have to use the bathroom. I would be standing there waiting, thinking, *Okay, are they done yet? I have to tinkle.* And then some person with a baritone voice would tell me, "You're gonna wait your turn," and I would be outside the stall saying to myself, *I gotta go.* But I quietly waited my turn.

It might sound funny now, but it was very frightening then. I was eighteen. Here I was having to go to the bathroom and some scary person was telling me, "You're gonna wait your turn," until they were done doing whatever sexual activity they were doing. It was horrible.

I quickly learned that the stories you hear about prison are true. You have to get someone to protect you. I didn't know that then. Most women who were like me—high-profile, smaller, or younger—needed protection.

I learned how to act very quickly. But I was there for only three days. I was soon shipped out to Albion.

Chapter Thirteen

ALBION

The day they brought me up to Albion, I was once again shackled, and this time put on a prison bus, and driven all the way to upstate New York—a ten-hour drive to the town of Albion, near Niagara Falls.

It was the same setup there with cots, not cells, because it was a medium-security facility and I was a medium-security prisoner. The guards called it "babysitting." They didn't consider the inmates in Albion hardcore criminals. They considered them just lowlifes who, for the most part, couldn't afford a good lawyer. A lot of the inmates, in fact, were homeless women who had been arrested for prostitution or for selling a vial of crack one too many times.

The living quarters were divided into three categories. The first part included the back buildings, H through N, which were built in the early '90s to accommodate overcrowding. These were huge dorms that resembled a homeless shelter. They housed about one hundred bunk beds (really two metal slabs, one on top of the other, with a piece of foam padding that they passed off as a mattress thrown on top) lined up and separated by a four-foot partition—the kind of cubicles they have in office buildings. This was where you would go when you entered the prison. If you had disciplinary infractions, you remained there. If you didn't have infractions, eventually you were told to pack up: you were moving "up the hill." Not me. I spent most of my seven years in those back building dorms.

"Up the hill" was part of the original prison built in the late 1800s. Three brick-style buildings housed dorms A, B, and C, which resembled the older projects found in inner cities. These buildings were quieter than the back buildings. When you first moved up the hill, you were put in a large room that was home to a dozen women at any given time. It might have been quieter than the back buildings, but there was absolutely zero privacy. The bathrooms and shower areas looked like props from a B-rated horror flick. Everything squeaked and creaked. There were so many layers of paint on the walls that as they peeled away what remained were just flakes of pea green, brown, and pale blue. These buildings were falling apart. I made it up there once and didn't consider it a reward for good behavior.

If an inmate could tough-out living dorm-style in buildings A, B, and C, they were eventually moved to a private room in one of these buildings or a building with all private rooms called the Annex.

The Annex was part of the main Administration Building at the front of the prison. There were fourteen private rooms on the first floor and fourteen on the second floor. During my last year at Albion I went straight from the back buildings to a private room in the Annex. Procedure would have been for me to spend a while in a twelve-bed dorm, but prison officials decided that might have been too risky. The A, B, and C dorms were in buildings that were not originally built as a prison, so they had a lot of closets, stairwells, and places to disappear if you so desired. Since I had charged that I had been attacked in a desolate stairwell of one of these buildings, the Department of Corrections decided not to take a chance that history would repeat itself.

The Mess Hall was built in the early '90s, also to accommodate the influx of new prisoners in the back buildings. It was a large, modern brick structure where inmates would grab a tray and wait on a line cafeteria-style. Each of the servers behind the counter, all prisoners, had a specific task. One would slop the potatoes on your tray, the next person would dump the meat, and so on. You'd take your tray and sit at the next available table in a row where a guard would direct you to sit. You'd eat your meal, and after about ten minutes a guard would dismiss the table. You were expected to return to your housing unit.

Solitary was located in a closed-off section of buildings A, B, and C. The Special Housing Unit (SHU) was attached to the Administration Building. This was where you were held for serious offenses like writing a letter to a guard. I did that once and received ninety days in solitary.

There were head counts right before lunchtime, dinner, and bedtime. It was like the Army—you had to stand at the foot of your bed and be accounted for—and I was not the Army type. It was a rude awakening for me.

On a routine day, you'd wake up by 8:00 A.M., go to work, break for lunch, and go back to work. After your eight-hour shift, all your time was yours to do with as you wished: sleep, watch TV, use the gym, etc. All meals were optional. I usually skipped dinner. Lights out was at 11:00 P.M.

Visiting days were only one day a week for about five hours, on a Saturday or Sunday. The inmates would walk up to the visitors' building and the guards would pat you down to make sure you weren't going in with any contraband. When visiting hours would end, all the inmates would sit there and one by one the women would be called in to be strip searched, which was the most degrading thing in the world.

The guard would stand there while you took off all your clothes and then tell you to bend over and "spread your cheeks" so they could look up your rectum. Can you imagine having this job? And they don't get paid nearly as much as a gynecologist or proctologist. They search inside your mouth and also tell you to lift your breasts (what am I going to hide under my breasts?). I think the whole point is to degrade you. The funny part is that drugs ran rampant in prison. The inmates would stick the drugs so far up their orifices that the guards would rarely detect them with their crude and cursory exams.

Despite the humiliating searches afterwards, having visitors was a nice diversion from the daily routine of prison life.

A routine day? That was the type of day I rarely had.

Inmates worked only five days a week, so on your two days off you usually wanted to relax, which was not happening because the guards kicked your bed at 8:00 A.M. You still had to be up and dressed—no sleeping, no lying around in your pj's. I didn't get a good night's sleep for seven years.

I was moved up to Albion to get me out of the New York metropolitan area—away from my family and the media. At that time anybody else in my situation would have stayed at Bedford Hills for a few years. I wouldn't have gone up to Albion until I had been in Bedford three or four years. But the Department of Corrections also wanted to move me away from my family to make my time harder. Back then, they would keep you in Bedford until you had about two years left on your sentence and then move you to Albion.

They figured it was easier to send me all the way to upstate New York, away from the center of the storm.

At Albion the guards were particularly cruel to me because they thought of me as a movie star, and they said that they were going to show me a thing or two to bring me down to Earth. The bizarre thing is that I never thought of myself as anything other than a regular inmate, but to them, the minute someone was on TV, they were a rich, snobby celebrity. They thought that if you were on the news, you were being paid for it. And my story and my face were all over the place. So they thought, here's this spoiled little rich girl from the suburbs, and she's on TV, and she gets all this attention and makes tons of money, and only just now is she finally paying for committing a crime.

To me, there is a very small distinction between a correction officer and a criminal. (It was no surprise that the shocking abuses committed by those soldiers in Abu Ghraib prison in Iraq were committed by some former U.S. correction officers, whose past charges had accused them of abuse over the years.) Many correction officers come from underprivileged or poor backgrounds, and those at Albion especially hated and resented me and made that very clear. I went days without eating while in solitary (for fabricated or minor disciplinary infractions), because the guards would urinate in my food or juice cups or give me spoiled milk, so that I wouldn't have anything to eat or drink.

They made their gross actions obvious and did not disguise them. They did not hide their disdain for a targeted prisoner. They wanted you to know exactly what they were doing. They did it on purpose to just add to the mental anguish. Then they'd say, "Oh, the little prima donna is complaining." They just tortured me. I'd sit there for days and not eat or drink anything.

There were people in prison with me who knew what the officers were doing, and they would save portions of their meals to give me some decent food. There were some nice women in there. They would save their milk and cereal and hide it and give it to me, because they would hear these officers in the hallways describing to each other what they did to me. Some of the women who were incarcerated in Albion with me thought what these officers were doing to me was disgusting and horrible. They felt very bad for me.

I kept wondering how I was going to survive the next two years. I was devastated. I didn't know what to do. I was constantly crying. I was terrified.

I didn't know if I was even going to make it. I would tell Eric Naiburg, and he would complain to Albion authorities, and then they would take me into "protective custody," which was the same as being locked up for breaking the rules. They locked me in The Cage/cell/hole/solitary twenty-four hours a day to punish me for complaining, and they wouldn't let me out. It was torturous.

Anyone in prison is powerless—young or old, rich or poor, it doesn't matter. You are at the mercy of the prison guards. They would lock me in The Cage whenever they wanted to.

The guards could do anything that they wanted. They could beat you up; they could urinate in your food; they could rape you. Abused women in society now have shelters they can escape to, but abused women in prison have nowhere to run. The guards control every aspect of a prisoner's life.

Men are tortured as well. If they don't like a male prisoner—a pedophile, for example—the guards let the other prisoners beat him up or kill him. That's how Jeffrey Dahmer died. That's how John Geoghan, the sixty-eight-year-old defrocked pedophile priest, was murdered in August 2003 in a Massachusetts prison. That's what they can do. The guards just turn their backs. You know: "Get 'em."

I was terrified of the correction officers.

But in prison you need to be concerned about the prisoners as well. In county jail I wasn't really afraid of the other prisoners because most of them were not heavy-duty criminals; they were there for very petty crimes. They were just down on their luck. The women in Bedford included murderers. The women in Albion were there for prostitution, hitting their husbands, or drugs. Many of them had been abused. Though they were not there for very serious crimes, they were often violent.

In prison you would probably prefer to be surrounded by a thousand murderers than ten drug addicts. It is a fact that women who kill are usually spur-of-the-moment killers who reacted suddenly to something like an act of domestic violence. I noticed that women in prison for murder tended to become quite reflective and often wanted to better and improve themselves. Usually quiet and reserved, they were the ones who tried to help others through new programs.

Drug addicts, who seemed to make up 90 percent of the population of Albion, were often street people who sold drugs, stole, and would do anything to get high. They committed so many offenses because of their addiction that they ended up spending most of their adult lives going in and out of Albion as if it were a second home. These people were scary. They were for the most part uneducated, often unpredictable, and prone to violence. Not violent where they wanted to deliberately murder someone, but violent where they were willing to fight or attack over petty things like not being able to watch the TV show of their choice.

Because of their drug problems, they became animal-like, trying to survive. I noticed that even when they were temporarily off the drugs, their mentality was still the same. If I were in charge of the prison, they would never be released unless they were completely cured. They have a disease, and when they are thrown back onto our streets, they prey on the innocent over and over again.

The inequities start on the most basic level. Starting with county jail, there are so many impoverished incarcerated people who, if they had possessed the resources I had (money, a high-profile attorney), wouldn't even be there. The injustices against the poor and disadvantaged in prison are absolutely outrageous. They didn't pay their traffic tickets, and the judge sends them to jail for two or three weeks. The average person would have just paid the fines and gone home. Inability to pay didn't make them criminals. They were just poor. It's a terrible cycle they were in.

I felt totally helpless and frightened in prison because I didn't know what the guards were going to do to me next. They would walk around calling me "the Long Island Lolita," "the prima donna," and if I was on one of the tabloid television programs or the news, they would find out and blast it through the whole prison so that all the inmates, everybody, could see it.

They would also find out if any of the Made-For-TV movies about me were being rerun, and they'd make sure they put it on in all the housing units. The inmates would then stand there and cheer and scream and make fun of me. That was in county jail and prison as well. I just wanted to die.

At Albion I can't tell you how many times I heard: "You were on TV. Wow."

It was very strange for me there. From the moment I arrived I was like a pop star walking into the mall. The minute I walked into this place everyone yelled, "Oh wow, there's Amy Fisher." People flocked around me to shake my hand and talk to me and ask me all about Joey and ask me to tell them how it "really" happened. And I was just standing in the doorway, frozen. I just didn't get it.

All that was going through my mind was, *I'm in prison, get the hell away from me,* which was the worst thing I could have thought, because then when I didn't sit there and engage in conversation and tell them my innermost thoughts, they would call me a "snobby bitch." And then they wanted to beat me up.

If I went to prison for life, I would be thinking of every way I could escape every single day. I don't know how people who get life terms resign themselves to that. I remember meeting people in prison who were in there for life and I would think, *How do they do this?* They sit there and they hope that all their appeals will come through, and they're still in denial.

I was sent to Albion a few days before Christmas 1992. The abuse started immediately. The moment I got there my belongings, toiletries, prison uniforms, bedding, etc., were tossed out of the back of a truck, and and I was ordered to lug those several bags, weighing probably forty pounds apiece, to my new residence, a housing unit two miles away.

The guards thought it was funny that I was struggling to carry the heavy, unwieldy bags. They would say things like, "Too bad Joey isn't here to help you," and, "Don't you wish your maid was here?"

They were telling me things I didn't understand till later on, like, "Don't worry, you'll be able to buy a maid soon enough," and, "You'll have a boyfriend again real soon whether you like it or not—the kind with a beard and a dress." I later learned they were implying I would be forced into lesbianism.

One of the guards finally grabbed my bags, threw them over his shoulder, and told his colleagues, "That's enough." I guess he felt bad for me; he told me the truck routinely drops the inmate's bags directly at the housing units. From the moment I arrived at Albion I was singled out to be tortured. I was a source of amusement.

I was in Albion for several days when I was told to report to B-block. No explanation was given. In Albion inmates walk freely with a handwritten pass, which is the same as the hall passes we all remember from high school. I reported to B-block and was told to see a Sergeant Schwartz.

He was doing paperwork and did not even look up when I entered the room. I stood there not knowing if I should sit or stand, speak or remain silent. His uniform intimidated me. Every time I looked at the guards it was a constant reminder that I had done something terribly wrong.

Sergeant Schwartz looked up after about a minute that seemed to last an eternity. Sternly, he told me to have a seat. He proceeded to ask me how I was getting along at

Albion, as if it were my first semester at Yale. Not sure what to say, I meekly replied, "Fine."

I was anything but fine. I felt isolated and alone, constantly replaying the events that had led me to this horrible place. I was so remorseful, but the remorse I felt wasn't nearly enough to make up for the enormous pain I had inflicted on Mary Jo. I had to pay in some way for my actions, and I assumed that I too would feel pain as my punishment. I could never have imagined just how much pain would come my way. Pain the human mind does not even imagine when anticipating hurt.

Sergeant Schwartz began to tell me how Albion worked. He was even-toned and matter-of-fact. He told me that for a lot of the guards it was exciting to have me there. They had never had a "celebrity" like me there before. Who did they think I was, I wondered at the time, Christie Brinkley? He told me many of the guards were just curious about me and would do stupid things like ask for my autograph. I was to try to be nice even if I didn't feel like it, he said, because I was now in their kingdom. He also told me there was much talk about how a lot of them were going to "teach me a lesson." Not because I committed a crime, but because I was viewed as a spoiled rich brat who never had a hard day in her life; they were going to show me what hard times were like.

At that point all the guards in uniform looked alike to me. I had no idea about ranks, like in the military or police force. Sergeant Schwartz informed me that, as a sergeant, he held a higher rank than an officer. He told me to try to comply with their orders, but if things got really bad I should tell him. He said he would try to look out for me. Why would this stranger want to look out for me? That thought left my mind as quickly as it had entered. It didn't matter if someone wanted to be nice — who was I to refuse help?

Life there was very bad, for years.

I was a kid who knew only the rules my parents and teachers had taught me. I was used to following the rules. The one time I made my own rules, look what happened. I wasn't very good at it.

The rules of Albion: I was told everybody gets a job and you work eight hours a day. You get paid $15 biweekly. You go to an office that is kind of like an employment agency where they have lists of all the jobs in the prison. They ask you about your skills and your education level, and they offer you a choice: do you want to work in place A or place B?

Well, I went to that office, and they determined that I was going to wash pots and pans in the cafeteria.

"Okay, but I have no choices?"

"No, you're Amy Fisher, you don't have any choices. This is what they want you to do." So they determined that they wanted me to be a slave. And I did it. I did it for eight hours a day, and they'd say, "You know what? We want you to work overtime. You'll sit here for fifteen hours and scrub these pots until your fingers fall off." And then if I objected, they'd punish me. They'd say, "Oh, the prima donna doesn't want to wash pots. We'll throw her in The Cage for two weeks."

And that's just what they did. I was eighteen and living in a cage because I broke the special unique rules they designed for me.

Looking back, I realize I gave them the reaction they were looking for. If I had kept my big mouth shut, worked the overtime, done whatever unreasonable thing they told me to do, and simply said, "Yes, sir," it would have been no fun for them to harass me. They would have moved on to someone more entertaining to torture.

The Cage: it's solitary. All by yourself. They drag you to this tiny little room, and they lock you up. And who knows what the guards have done to your food.

If you were fortunate enough to get a window, the view was of a brick wall. All you had to sleep on was a foam mattress, which was just like a piece of padding. There was a toilet-sink combination. In Albion guards were 80 percent male. They looked through the big glass part of the door and watched female prisoners when they used the bathroom. This is sick. Some did it for sexual reasons; some did it just to humiliate the prisoner. I would not go to the bathroom, or I would time it so that as soon as they walked by I ran to the toilet. It is disgusting that the Department of Corrections allowed this. This was straight-out abuse. And it still occurs throughout our country in women's prisons.

There were so many times I would ask myself, *How did this happen to me?*

I knew the rule was that you worked eight hours and then you were done. I followed that rule. But fifteen hours? Why were they doing this to me? I didn't understand that. They kept saying that they hated me just because of who I was. And I kept saying, "This isn't fair," and it took me a while to realize, *You know what? Life isn't fair.* Yes, they were awful people, and yes, it was easier to just do it than try to say, "Hey, I did what I'm supposed to do, I'm a fair person, you'll be fair too." They were in charge, and they were the bosses, and they were not fair. It took me many years to realize that; while I was in there being tortured, it was hard to learn anything.

Prison life is simple. Everyone has to wake up at a certain time and eat at a certain time. Well, everybody else did, but they didn't do that with me. They would kick my bed five, six times during the middle of the night. They would wake me up. They wouldn't let me sleep. They were very, very malicious to me. But more than that, their actions were in total violation of Department of Corrections rules and were against the law. The problem was that no one cared what rules the authorities broke while making my life hell.

When I reported it, they would tell me, "Stop being a spoiled brat and shut up." It was just unbelievable. I shunned attention, but I could not get away from it.

Albion has spacious property, with a fence surrounding it, and when I walked around outside the buildings, with two thousand other women, mobs of people would yell to me, "Amy Fisher! You were on TV." "Amy Fisher, I saw your movie." "Amy Fisher, tell me the real story about Joey." And all I wanted was to be left alone.

There were people there who were nice to me, but I didn't really have any close friendships. I didn't tell people my innermost thoughts, but hey, I did learn how to play card games!

I didn't socialize much. Mostly because I was locked in The Cage so often that after a while it had become so routine that the guards would even let me pack my own bags. (The guards were supposed to pack inmates' bags.)

There was one period when I was in The Cage for a month, and when I was released, after only two hours I was put back in for another month. I was put in The Cage, by the way, for hemming my prison-issue pants, which were too long to walk around in safely. You are not allowed to alter prison property, but my pants were too long, and I'd trip on them.

I spent about three of my seven years in prison in The Cage, in solitary.

I had this reputation in the media for being an incorrigible prisoner. Everyone thought I was getting in fights and disobeying every major rule.

Not true — my behavior there was not that dramatic. I would get in trouble and be thrown in The Cage for things like having my fingernails too long. They used to come in and measure my nails with a ruler. Prisoners couldn't dye their hair. I used to try to dye my hair with their lye soap. If you mixed their lye soap with peroxide, it colored your hair. To think, people wash with this. And they'd complain, "She dyed her hair. Time to lock her in The Cage. She's a bad inmate."

They didn't want anyone to alter her image, as if they wouldn't recognize me, locked in there, with lighter-colored hair. They referred to it as trying to change one's identity. I wish it were that easy.

At that point I didn't care about being locked away. Sometimes I actually needed the rest, to go sit there in The Cage and not be bothered for weeks. I actually did it on purpose a few times. For things like the fingernails and the hair I was in there only a week or two. Other times it was for many months at a time. I had some peace being alone in there.

Imagine sitting in a walk-in closet, closing the door, and not being permitted to emerge for three months. You'd have your clothes hanging around you, shoes lined up on the floor, and maybe some makeup left on a shelf. No television, perhaps a book or two that are supposed to entertain you for months. Boredom. This is what being locked up in The Cage is like in a women's prison.

When I was locked up, I had nothing better to do than apply my makeup countless times, trying new techniques and colors each time. With nothing but time on your hands in prison, and especially in solitary, there's not much to do besides reflect and read and work on your appearance. I would sit for endless hours plucking my leg hairs out one by one with tweezers. I have to say, it's the smoothest my legs have ever been, though I don't keep up this practice now. *Why bother shaving,* I thought, *when I have all this extra time.*

I've heard that women who pluck their body hairs with tweezers suffer from some kind of neurosis. I'm not sure what kind exactly, but at best, it is considered strange. I guess it does seem odd unless you're locked in a room for months with nothing else to do.

I was so bored that I actually felt like I was losing my mind. I suppose psychological torture was just what the Department of Corrections had in mind when it implemented this form of punishment.

They had weird rules about what you could wear and how you could look in prison. We were allowed to wear our own tops, shoes, and makeup. They supplied us with green bellbottom pants or a green skirt or dress.

While I was in prison, it did not look like there would be a happy ending for me. I just wanted to die. I was so embarrassed about what I had done. I had very few friends at that point, because all my friends back home were around my age and their parents were saying, "I don't want you to see her. You can't talk to her. Don't call or accept calls from her."

I would phone a friend, and her mother would scream at me, "Don't call my house anymore," and hang up on me. And when I was in prison, everybody else went on to live their own lives.

Many friends did support me at first. When I left for prison, they would promise, "I'll write you. I'll keep in touch." But as one year changed into the next — and I was there seven years — we lost contact. The late teens and early twenties are a very transitional point in people's lives: they go to college, they graduate, they land their first job, they find their first real boyfriend. Later they were even getting married, and I was still sitting in prison, frozen in time as a teenager.

I never had those experiences. All I knew was high school. Well, do you think a twenty-three-year-old woman who just graduated from college and is working at her first job on Wall Street wants to talk about high school with someone serving time in prison? You just drift apart. These friends and I really had nothing in common anymore. Amy was just the sad young girl who went to jail—we feel bad for her, but our lives moved on.

Although I was off my friends' radar, I was the center of attention at Albion, and that held true from my first day.

I had been in Albion about a week when three movies about me were released. They aired on all three major networks, and two on the same night. That's never happened before.

The one starring Alyssa Milano was based on the Buttafuocos' perspective on me as a lying, obsessed, wild, out-of-control vixen who *might* have said hello to Joey once. The one starring Drew Barrymore was supposed to be objective, and Noelle Parker starred in the one that was supposedly my story, but it portrayed a long, torrid love affair, which wasn't true. None were realistic. The three movies were so completely different that I often said they should have just aired *Sybil*, the film about a woman with multiple personalities, instead.

There I was upstate, in prison for only a week, lying on my little cot, reading a book, and of course, every housing unit had to play those Amy Fisher movies. All the prisoners were flipping back and forth between the channels during the commercials, just because they didn't want to miss any part of any movie—they wanted to see every minute of all three. That was a fiasco with repercussions for weeks.

"Amy, I saw your movie."

"Amy, you're so famous."

That was the last thing I wanted. I just wanted to crawl in a hole and become invisible.

And then, of course, they all thought I had to have millions of dollars because I was now a TV character, and people wanted and demanded money from me. When I told them I didn't have millions of dollars, they called me a liar. It was impossible, they thought. It was really hard for me.

I turned inward. I tried to better myself in prison. I constantly reflected on what I had done to Mary Jo and what had led me to that. Even today there isn't a day that goes by when I don't think about this.

I sat for hours, days, weeks, and years on end, trying to figure out how to reconcile what I had done and how to straighten out my life. I knew that furthering my education was one step.

When Mario Cuomo was the governor of New York, the prevailing theory was that if you take prisoners and educate them and then they re-enter society, they can get real jobs if they have a college education.

Governor George Pataki came into office in 1994 with the credo: Why educate the criminals? They don't deserve it—not bothering to realize how education can keep many former criminals from reverting back to their old ways. He pulled all types of funding for college education. In fact, as an inmate, you couldn't even pay for it yourself through the state if you wanted to. You were basically not allowed to be educated.

He was, in effect, taking this opportunity away from all these people, most of them nonviolent offenders, who were in prison for selling drugs and committing petty crimes, like robbery, to get money because they had no education to earn a decent living. Instead of educating them so they didn't have to commit crimes to sustain themselves, they were warehousing them to send them right back onto those streets where they had no choice but to keep re-offending because they had no other way to earn a living. It was just a vicious cycle, and Pataki was shortsighted for doing this. It just doesn't make sense that he wasn't helping to rehabilitate these people.

The inmate college program Pataki did away with had been funded by the state. Eventually I was able to work through college correspondence classes that my mother had to pay a lot of money for me to do. (I had taken my high school final exams and earned my high school diploma while I was in Nassau County Jail, when I was first arrested in 1992.)

For years I read a lot and worked diligently on my college courses. I was on the path to bettering myself, despite the resistance from the penal system. And despite overtime shifts washing dishes.

My work experience in prison was equally frustrating. I would repeatedly get different jobs, including Porter I, Porter II, Laundry Operator, Painter Helper, Hospital Porter, Block Porter, and Groundskeeper. If you were unhappy with your assignment, you could write a letter to a committee and they would set up an appointment for you where they gave you a list of all the other jobs. The only difference between my request and those of other inmates was that I was only allowed to do jobs that required hard physical labor. Keep in mind that I had a high school diploma, which many of the prisoners did not possess.

"Do you want to be a landscaper?"

"Do you want to be a painter?"

"Do you want to be a housecleaner?"

Inmates were supposed to be able to pick the job that their skills best suited them for. Not Amy Fisher, though.

I constantly complained about the hard work and long hours in the kitchen, and they finally let me out after I refused to work those extra hours so many times that the officials realized that I spent more time in The Cage than I spent with the pots and pans. They let me out of the kitchen, but they put me in something called the Storehouse, where you lifted seventy-five-pound boxes of fish. I had to roll the boxes which weighed almost as much as I did. It was ridiculous. I was a one-hundred-pound little girl, and they were telling me to lift these seventy-five-pound boxes.

The funny thing was that if you had a GED or a high school diploma, as I did, they were supposed to place you in an office job. Again, not me. They insisted that I do hard labor. But when they realized that I couldn't physically do the Storehouse work, they sent me to work on the Paint Crew, painting the inside of the buildings. Then it was on to the Lawns & Grounds Crew, which meant breaking up ice and shoveling snow in the cold upstate New York winter and mowing lawns with a manual mower in the blisteringly hot summers.

Since I had a high school diploma, I was the only one qualified to operate the tractor, which was used as a snowplow in the winter (even at 3:00 A.M.), so at least I was able to keep my feet warm.

Although they gave me the Lawn & Grounds job as a punishment, I was able to feel somewhat alive working outdoors, with a bit more freedom to wander around. (If you had a Lawn & Grounds uniform, you had a free pass to walk around the property.) I would steal precious moments to just sit and think or study outside without the clamor of the prison as a distraction.

Sometimes when I had that job, since there were so many acres of hills and trees around, I would walk around peacefully raking leaves. I remember strolling around aimlessly by myself with my little bag and my rake. I'd feel almost like I was in a park. There was nobody behind me to yell at me or even talk to me. I would only hear leaves blowing back and forth, and I'd think, Oh God, only to be free.

This has got to be what it's like to be free.

LEFT: April 1994 visit with my mom at Albion.

BELOW LEFT:
My mother and I at a 1995 visit at Albion.

BELOW: During my six-month stay in The Cage at Albion, at the height of my abuse in prison. (1996)

LEFT:
With my mom at Albion in 1996 during my darkest days there.

RIGHT:
With my mom at Albion in 1996.

ABOVE:
December 1997 visit from Mom in
Albion.

ABOVE:
Me in Albion in 1997.

LEFT:
Me and my mom
in 1998 at Albion.

Chapter Fourteen

A BRIEF REPRIEVE

I was free from Albion—briefly.

In September 1993, I was brought down to Bedford Hills again, this time for three months, to wait until they needed me to go to Nassau County to appear at Joey Buttafuoco's Statutory Rape sentencing.

In Albion I was the most notorious of the prisoners. But at Bedford Hills there were several women who also had well-known histories. It was a nice reprieve to not be the center of attention.

These women were an interesting group. Some I made friends with, others were very cold to me. One of the nicest women I met there was Marie La Pinta, to whom I dedicated this book. Perhaps one of the most infamous was Pamela Smart, the New Hampshire schoolteacher who hired a student (who was also her lover) to kill her husband. She was serving a life sentence in New York because she was too high profile in New Hampshire and she'd had so many problems there that they weren't equipped to deal with her. She's in Bedford for life with no chance of parole. She told me about this appeal and that appeal, and she was still saying she didn't commit the crime. Whether she did it or not, I thought, *Whoa, is she in denial? She's never getting out.* It's nearly impossible to win an appeal, especially if you have received negative national attention in the media.

I felt bad for her, but she didn't feel bad for herself, because she was in such denial. She was adamant about her innocence.

I lived in the same housing unit with her for three months until I was transferred back to Albion. It may sound strange, but the thing I remember most about her was her addiction to Diet Pepsi.

She was the "star" of the housing unit, which was fine by me. She took the attention away from me.

Both inmates and guards were constantly whispering about every move she made. She had no peace. I found her to be a warm and friendly person. I liked her. It's odd to know what she probably did and still like her, but I did, even though she was the "Joey" in her case—an adult encouraging a young smitten kid to commit a crime against a spouse.

She was depicted in the press as a sort of seductress who preyed upon teenage boys. A cold vamp who had her husband killed. She may be where she belongs, or she may not, but either way, she was a likable woman. Her situation has always seemed to me like a mirror image of my own.

Laurie Kellogg was convicted of hiring hit men to kill her abusive husband. She asked me about TV movies and began talking to me about offers she was getting from networks for the rights to her story. She wasn't sure if she should participate. I later saw *Lies of the Heart: The Story of Laurie Kellogg* on the USA network. I guess she thought it was a good idea after all.

I couldn't help but feel sorry for her. She had two small boys who would come visit her and cry when they had to leave. It was heartbreaking. Some of her harsher critics said she should have thought about her boys before having her husband murdered. A person thinking logically probably would have, but she was a victim of severe abuse. It's hard to be logical when subjected to abuse in your own home.

Carolyn Warmus was another notorious prisoner whom I shared time with. She was an upstate New York elementary school teacher and the daughter of a millionaire who was convicted of killing her lover's wife. As with me, Laurie Kellogg, and Pam Smart, she also had movies made about her life—*A Murderous Affair: The Carolyn Warmus Story* and *The Dangers of Love*.

She obviously didn't handle incarceration well. She was always doped up on mental health medication. She was the first one on line for those prescriptions. She wore the same prison-issue pants and sweatshirt every day, in spite of the fact that she was from a well-off family. She wore no makeup and mumbled to herself a lot. I never spoke to her, though she let it be known that she "hated" me.

Judy Clark was serving a seventy-five-year sentence for the 1981 hijacking of a Brinks truck that left three dead when she was a member of the radical Weather Underground. She was very into helping others around her in prison. She started a program called ACE to help inmates deal with the AIDS epidemic, which runs rampant in the prison system. She was also in charge of the prenatal program and the children's center. It was hard to imagine that she could have participated in anything that left three people dead. She spent every waking moment of her time in prison helping to improve the quality of life of those around her. She tried to get me a job working in the children's center in 1993, but I was rejected. Amy Fisher was deemed unsuitable to nurture, read to, or play with children.

Clark's fellow radical Kathy Boudin was not as nice to me as Clark was. She was very standoffish and much more interested in associating with the downtrodden than with someone she perceived to be a spoiled, bratty suburbanite.

This is a portion of a column I wrote in the *Long Island Press* about Kathy Boudin when she was released on probation in October 2003:

REFLECTIONS ON KATHY BOUDIN

I lived in a prison block with Kathy Boudin for several months back in the early '90s. She had been sentenced to 20 years to life for the 1981 armored-car heist in Rockland County that left three members of law enforcement dead. She was part of the radical activist group the Weather Underground, and was driving, unarmed, in the enclosed cab of the U-Haul truck used as the getaway vehicle during the robbery.

In prison, not surprisingly, this 1960s radical was still fighting for the underdog. From initiating support programs that helped people cope with AIDS to developing a program which helped incarcerated mothers maintain relationships with their children, Boudin was perceived as the consummate healer by the less fortunate. Earning her master's degree in adult education while in prison, she then helped write a handbook to assist inmates with children in foster care in coping with their situation. I duly noted her accomplishments and optimistic attitude toward helping others, and thought Boudin would be an inspiration.

Not knowing much about Boudin at the time, or even why she was in prison, I had no idea about her outlook on Caucasians and people of relative privilege. I did not realize I would be disliked because of the color of my skin or my upper-middle-class background. Boudin, who is white, said it best herself at her parole hearing: "I had a framework that said, essentially, white people, because of having privileges, are essentially bad."

Although I lived with Boudin for a while, she made it clear that I was not welcome in her world.

Her co-defendant Judy Clark, on the other hand, was much warmer and more embracing. She, like Boudin, was driven by political passion. Clark was one of the shooters and was sentenced to 75 years to life. Clark felt betrayed by Boudin. She, like others, believed Boudin received leniency because Boudin's father was a big-time lawyer, and that Boudin had much more involvement than she was admitting.

Boudin, now 60, is finally being paroled on Oct. 1, 2003, after 22 years behind bars. Having denied Boudin parole twice in the last two years, the drastic reversal of the parole board is surprising. Just this past May, the board decided that Boudin's achievements in prison were clearly outweighed by the serious nature of her crime. In August, though, the board praised her achievements during her incarceration and concluded that she had "done so much time." The reason for the abrupt turnaround is not clear. Perhaps it's because Judge David Ritter, who imposed a sentence of 20 years to life on Boudin, concluded, "I see no reason in the world why Miss Boudin should not be paroled at the expiration of the 20 years."

I'd like to believe Boudin is being released because the parole board realized she is not beyond redemption.

When Governor Pataki took office in 1994, he vowed he would be tough on violent offenders. There would be no special cases, no exceptions. It's refreshing to see the parole board finally break away from his lock-'em-up, throw-away-the-key attitude. Now we have to sit back and see if the two parole board members who granted Boudin's release are removed from appointment, or if other board members will muster the guts in other cases to follow their courageous lead. There are many like Boudin who committed terrible acts, yet over the years have become remorseful and tried to contribute to society as much as possible from behind bars.

Freeing Boudin does not diminish the horrific crime in which she participated. Lives were lost and families destroyed. Nothing can undo that damage. However, condemning Boudin to a life of incarceration means that our society doesn't believe people can be rehabilitated, that they can change.

Personally, I don't agree with many of Kathy Boudin's ideals. However, it is apparent to anyone apprised of her many accomplishments and passive nature that Boudin will, without doubt, re-enter our free world and strive to make it a better place. She is an intelligent, highly educated woman with a social conscience. She's had 22 years to think about her crimes and mistakes. She will have to live with those demons. That punishment is her real life sentence.

I had never met anyone like Boudin before, someone who held such strong political beliefs, someone whose politics kept her from associating with me.

Another notorious prisoner who disliked me, but not for idealistic reasons, was Jean Harris, the uptight, upper-crust, then-seventy-year-old school headmistress who killed her lover, Dr. Herman Tarnower, creator of *The Scarsdale Diet*. She was perhaps one of the best-known Bedford prisoners. Some inmates told me that they thought she didn't like the idea that someone new would be diverting all the attention from her. As I was entering Bedford Hills in December 1992 to start my prison sentence, Harris was finishing hers. She was granted clemency by then Governor Cuomo and scheduled to be free within days.

One would think that Harris, who was one of the most well-known female inmates in New York, would have been more open-minded and compassionate than most people. Surprisingly, she was not. I had been in Bedford a day or two when she walked up to me, as I ate in the cafeteria, with all the muster of a nursing home attendant and started telling me I wasn't special. (As if that was what I was thinking as I ate my Farina.) She continued berating me, saying that I was an inmate like everybody else and there would be no free rides for me. I had no idea who she was until she walked away and all the women at my table told me to ignore that crazy old Jean Harris. As the years passed and I endured unwanted attention because of my notoriety, I couldn't help but think back on Harris' lack of compassion and understanding.

Before I knew it, my three months at Bedford had come to an end.

LEFT:
My father visiting me in September 1993 at Bedford Prison when I returned to testify against Joey.

Chapter Fifteen

TESTIFYING AGAINST JOEY

I didn't want to go back to Nassau County to appear in court at Joey's Statutory Rape sentencing. I didn't care what happened to Joey. I had no desire to read a victim impact statement. Although everyone said I was vindicated, I didn't want the publicity. It wasn't going to change my circumstances.

There were cameras in my face wherever I went, and I was in chains, feeling every bit like the degraded criminal I was. I also didn't want to go to Nassau County Jail, where I would be thrown in a disgusting small cell once again like a forgotten animal for twenty-three hours a day with no soap, no clean underwear, no clothes, no pillow, no warm blanket, not even a real bed—just a one-quarter piece of padded foam on a metal slab like the ones they perform autopsies on. And then there was the small amount of slop they referred to as food that wasn't fit to feed a pig in a pen. (And for this they pay Nassau County Jail "cooks" close to $100,000 a year.)

All of this was not worth it for me to add my two cents at Joey's sentencing. The damage had already been done. I now had some insight into what Mary Jo must have felt about me—and this was the guy who set all this in motion. I did not want to see him.

Eric Naiburg arranged for me to go, and I was annoyed. I had no control. I was put in chains and led around like a circus freak. I was escorted into the courtroom in handcuffs to read my statement. My handcuffs were removed for the hundreds of viewers in the room. I was humiliated and uncomfortable.

Here are some portions of my statement:

> Before I begin, I would like to thank Your Honor for permitting me this opportunity to address the Court. I am doing so not only because I hope it will be of some assistance to the Court, but also because for me it represents closure, an end to the darkness of these past years...

> Approximately one year ago, I stood before another Judge of the Court and was sentenced to five to fifteen years in state prison. At that sentencing, I told Judge Goodman that two things were true...that I had an affair with a married man and that that married man was aware of my intentions toward his wife and encouraged me. Those things were as true then as they are today. That married man was the Defendant, Joseph Buttafuoco.

Since I first uttered those truths, Joseph Buttafuoco publicly labeled me crazy, psychopathic, depraved, and unworthy of belief. I was the subject of a Made-For-TV movie, inspired by Mr. Buttafuoco, which portrayed me as an obsessed teenager fantasizing a relationship with an older married man true to his marital and moral vows.

These proclamations and denials continued until six weeks ago, when he stood before this Court and admitted, for all the world to hear, that I was not some deranged teenager fantasizing a relationship, a relationship which ended in devastating consequences for all concerned. He has finally told part of the truth.

I know and believe that he entered the plea of guilty because he was, in fact, guilty. I know and believe that he entered the plea of guilty because the evidence against him was overwhelming. I know and believe that he entered the plea because even Joseph Buttafuoco could no longer deny the truth.

I know and believe that he entered his plea because he was aware that the District Attorney had in his possession numerous motel receipts, signed by Mr. Buttafuoco, his signature verified by the FBI. One of those receipts he learned contained his New York State driver's license number, and one, the license plate number of his wife's car, a car he used to take me to motels. He was aware, Your Honor, that I had accurately described the inside of his boat and the inside of an apartment he kept over his place of business...my description having been verified by the District Attorney. He knew, before he entered his plea, that numerous witnesses had finally come forward and testified to his incessant bragging concerning the sexual relationship he was having with a sixteen-year-old teenager. He was aware, and is aware, that I accurately described unique physical markings which only a person who had been intimate with him would know. He was aware of the numerous witnesses who saw us together and the phone records corroborating our illicit activities. These things and more, he was aware of when he entered his plea of guilty. He is aware, more than anyone else, of the lengthy, intense, and ultimately devastating relationship that began when I was a sixteen-year-old with braces.

Your Honor, when this relationship began, I was not just a sixteen-year-old teenager taken to bed by a man close to twice my age. I was a sixteen-year-old teenager that was shown a world I was not ready for, a world of elaborate spending and fast boats. A world of expensive restaurants and cheap motels. He taught me well. He taught me to disrespect myself and deceive my parents. Unfortunately, these were lessons I too quickly learned…

I am permitted to stand here because the law gives me that right. I am exercising that right not because I want to be vindictive, and not because I want to say to the world, "I told you so." I am exercising that right because I want to finally close the door on the horror of the past years. I am exercising that right because I want to see that justice is done to the limited extent available to this Court. I am exercising that right so that maybe one other teenage girl might be spared the pain, the devastation, and the loss of self-respect that such a relationship inevitably brings.

For the past year I have been imprisoned. Prison is at best a difficult and unnatural world. When you sit alone in your cell at night, you must reflect...and I do reflect. When I reflect on the pain I caused Mrs. Buttafuoco, her children, and my own family, I can accept and understand my imprisonment. However, when I consider the chain of events which ultimately motivated and encouraged my actions, it is far more difficult to understand. I know and believe that had Mr. Buttafuoco permitted me to cross the bridge between adolescence and adulthood unmolested, I would not be where I am today. I do not offer this as an excuse. There is no excuse. I simply offer it for the Court's consideration.

When I was preparing these remarks, I obviously considered what request I would make of this Court. My first thoughts were that I would ask that Mr. Buttafuoco be sentenced to more than the six months promised in view of the fact that this Statutory Rape led to consequences far greater and more devastating than the abuse of a young girl. At times I considered telling the Court that I don't care, that I have gone far beyond the desire for vengeance, simply wanting to get on with my life. Ultimately, I have decided that neither of those approaches is fitting or appropriate.

I am asking this Court to punish Mr. Buttafuoco as this Court sees fit, as justice, considering everything that has transpired, would mandate. I am not asking for me. I am asking on behalf of the message it will send to other teenagers who might be tempted by the glitter of the likes of Mr. Buttafuoco. And I am asking for it as a warning to other Joseph Buttafuocos who might exploit the naïveté of youth for their own purposes. I am confident that this Court understands, and that justice will be done.

Joey Buttafuoco was sentenced to six months for Statutory Rape.

Chapter Sixteen

BACK AT ALBION

I read my statement and was escorted out and shipped right back to Bedford Hills, where they had my possessions already packed, waiting for me to be put in a van to return to Albion within ten minutes.

I was shocked. Once I was back at Bedford, I had assumed I would be spending the reminder of my time there because Eric told me I would. That was another thing he told me that wasn't true.

I cried for the whole ten-hour ride back to Albion, handcuffed and shackled, in the backseat, with an officer on either side of me. I rode in silence, in tears, for the whole trip.

Back at Albion, the hard-labor work situation continued for the next six years. Eventually, near the end of my term, they let me do clerical work for half the day and Lawns & Grounds for the other half. But it took them all that time to let me do it. Six years of strenuous activity. I had muscles. I could have done an exercise video.

Even after all this time it is hard to forget prison. I went through so much in there. Even though Lawns & Grounds provided me with some brief periods of peace, it was still very hard work. In the summer I would mow the grass up and down hills in ninety-degree weather. And in the winter I was out there in ten-below temperatures, shoveling snow at all hours of the day and night. They would often wake me up at two or three o'clock in the morning to go shovel snow because the grounds had to be cleared. Some of the things they made me do, the ways they devised to torture me, were crazy. They were, for the most part, a sadistic bunch.

I believe everybody should be treated with dignity and respect. A prisoner who commits a crime should be incarcerated, and at least an attempt at rehabilitation should be made. I think the system should be one where everybody has a productive job. That's important, because inmates shouldn't just lie around doing nothing. They should be up and around and doing something worthwhile besides making their bed and practicing good hygiene—those are important things. But I think that these correction officers, these little cogs in the system, are not there to help rehabilitate the prisoner. And after all, besides punishment, that's the greater purpose of what prison is all about.

Think about it. Who would want to be a correction officer? Why would you want to do that? You sit in a prison with a bunch of lowlifes, half of whom have AIDS and other horrible diseases. They spit at you, they throw feces at you, and you want to sit and work among these people? If you were an idealistic person with a social worker mentality who wanted to help society, then I could understand it. But that is not the motive of most prison guards. It's not a job like going to an office or working at McDonald's. Think of the mentality of many of the people who work in there. Not all of them, but a lot of them. They take jobs as guards to feel powerful.

They were just plain sadistic. They'd tell you specific things that they found in your chart which they examined to find your weaknesses. If they discovered that an inmate they didn't like had AIDS, for example, they would tell everybody so that she would become a pariah.

It's hard to implement a productive system when you have these cogs working in there who are really no better than the criminals. The current system sounds good in theory. But it doesn't work that way.

People should absolutely be punished for crimes they commit, but there are degrees of punishment. They should be treated humanely. If you lock criminals in a cage, well, yes, they may be punished temporarily, but how is that going to benefit society when they're released?

You have to teach people how to be productive, especially people who come into the system without skills. You have to teach them how to function in society. And rehabilitation is as important as punishment, if not more. Would you want someone who spent twenty years in The Cage coming back and walking in your neighborhood? Or would you want someone who went to prison, was treated with respect, educated, rehabilitated, and taught how to function back in the streets?

I don't think I ever had a good day in prison. I had days of peace, however, when nobody was trying to kill me or make me miserable.

There were some inmates who were crazy who tried to harm me. One woman kept making sexual advances toward me and was continuously threatening me. One night when I was asleep she beat me on the head with a combination lock wrapped in a sock. And although I had bruises, since no one admitted they had witnessed it, nothing came of it. Why did she hurt me? Because I wouldn't have sex with her. She thought I rejected her because I thought I was better than her. I rejected her because I just wasn't interested. Other inmates wanted to beat me up because I didn't want to give them autographs.

It was very predatory in prison. Eventually Governor Pataki lowered the age an individual could enter an adult prison, in effect widening the pool of susceptible victims. These kids were just getting devoured. It was outrageous and devastatingly sad. When I was leaving the prison, I remember this little sixteen-year-old girl coming into Albion. It was a travesty. What they did to her was just horrible. These women, they'd intimidate her into having sex, they'd steal all her food.

Your family was allowed to send you things from the outside, kind of like sleepaway camp, but whatever you had—cookies, cigarettes, cheese balls—these predators would just steal everything. Your family was allowed to send you your own underwear and pajamas, and a lot of these women were street people who had nothing, so they would take everything they could. They did it to me too when I first got there.

If some of the more disadvantaged prisoners saw that your mother sent you a package of Oreos, they wanted them. And if you told them no, they would beat you up and take them anyway.

And there was nothing you could do about it.

Especially if you were me. The guards would say, "Well, call your mommy and tell her to buy you more." And they'd laugh at me.

Chapter Seventeen

PRISON RELATIONSHIPS

At least I was lucky that the women weren't raping me in prison, because that happened to a lot of other people. But that didn't happen to me. I don't know why. Maybe I was just lucky in that respect.

Many of the women in prison would find one of the hormonally challenged women to protect them, and they would become their girlfriends. I just couldn't muster that one.

Getting sexually involved with a woman in order to be protected? That I could not handle—especially the ones who looked and acted like men. I would have rather ended up dead. Although some sleazy tabloids ran stories by "former jailhouse lovers," it simply was not true that I was sexually involved with other female inmates.

Although I couldn't protect myself from the guards, I was able to find a way to protect myself from other prisoners. There were times when there were women who liked me and were my friends, and they would tell predatory inmates, "She's my girlfriend, don't bother her," just to protect me. But they weren't really my girlfriends.

If someone asked, I would respond, "Yeah, yeah, that's my girlfriend," because I didn't want to be bothered.

There were some tough inmates at Albion, so it became a good idea to have protection. I would cook, for example, and these tough women would come in and just laugh at me and throw my pots off to the side and begin cooking. If someone tough was your girlfriend, they'd think twice.

This having-a-girlfriend deal in prison was very funny. Most of the "relationships" these women were having in prison were not even sexual. They would just call each other girlfriends and hold hands. Women desire a different kind of closeness, an emotional one, than the physical relationships men find in prison.

Instead of sexual favors, I gave other inmates material things. Then they'd say they were my girlfriend for me and I'd be safe. I sought out the older women who were respected for their supposed intellect. A GED was a big deal there.

Sometimes someone would come up to me and say, "Your girlfriend is cheating on you." I'd just laugh.

They'd ask, "Don't you care?"

I'd answer, "You know how it goes. That's life."

I used to read papers like the *National Enquirer* that would run stories about "Amy's Lesbian Prison Lovers." They were pure fiction, and pretty outrageous. One tabloid ran a story that Pam Smart and I were "lesbian lovers." At the time I was in Albion, and Smart was in Bedford. The tabloid couldn't even properly research where I was at the time.

Some of the inmates would steal my ID cards or steal my photos of my mom or me and say, "Yeah, I knew Amy. She gave me this photo," or, "She was my lover. She gave me these photos as a token of our love," and they'd get to make some quick money. I was a commodity, and everyone tried to exploit me. Some of these women who claimed to be my prison lovers were horribly repulsive women with drug problems, and their lies about me were taken as The Truth.

As bad as that was, at this point I could deal with the prisoners and the tabloids—it was the guards who tortured me there for seven years. They never let up. Never.

I was constantly being sexually harassed. There were some correction officers who would sit and talk to each other, and I'd be sitting in a corner, and they'd be laughing at me, pointing at me, saying sexual things about me. It was terrible. It was like a nightmare where I was stuck in this horrible situation and nobody would help me.

There were a lot of correction officers there who were curious about me and wanted to get to meet the wild Amy Fisher they had heard about on TV and read about in the newspapers. Some would go to shocking lengths to "learn" more about me.

Chapter Eighteen

A LITTLE DIVERSION

At a certain point about three years into my stay at Albion, and going on for about four years, there was a correction officer whom I liked, and he liked me. He was very kind to me, and he basically let the prisoners know that if anyone did anything to me, they'd be in trouble with him. So I think that had a lot to do with my not having an extraordinary amount of problems with other inmates.

He really did protect me from the other prisoners. The inmates were afraid of anybody with that badge. So he had some power there. If somebody bothered me, he would just stop her in her tracks, using psychology by explaining that what they were doing wasn't a nice thing to do. The inmates soon felt that they should not mess with Amy, because Amy's officer friend was "going to get you." It was such a joke because he never bothered anyone. Since correction officers were so mean, the inmates thought every single guard was mean. It was ironic, because he was so nice and never tried to make anyone miserable.

He knew that the other guards were abusing me, but he couldn't stop it because the other guards weren't afraid of him. I used to cry all the time. He used to try to subtly talk to them, but there was only so much he could say.

And going to the authorities? Who was going to believe the Long Island Lolita?

The guards would say: "She's a spoiled brat. She has mental problems. Look, she shot somebody. She's in jail. And I'm an upstanding correction officer who goes to work and does what I'm supposed to do every day and goes home to my wife and kids. So who are you going to believe?"

Our relationship was very different from the relationships I had with the other officers there. I was going to college in prison at the time, and he used to help me with my homework. I was doing a lot of literature studies, reading a bunch of books and writing papers—many papers. And he'd help me study. He was more into education than the average correction officer, or hack. He actually read books! He was also higher up in the ranks. He wasn't just a run-of-the-mill guard.

This man was really kind to me. He would also flirt with me. By that I mean intense stares like he wanted to just reach out and touch me. He would wink at me when he thought no one was looking. I trusted him. I liked the attention. I did not have the maturity back then to understand that I was in prison and he was a guard and his flirtation was inappropriate and my receptiveness to it was equally inappropriate. It was nothing more than friendship to me.

One day I wanted to talk to him when he wasn't around. Somehow he always made me feel better. There was no particular reason for this; it's not like I had a deep relationship with him or he did anything to dramatically improve my pitiful prison existence. But conversation with a reasonably intelligent person made my mind drift out of prison toward the real world, even if only for a short time.

I wrote him a letter. It was harmless and innocent, basically telling him I missed his company. Prison made me vulnerable, and my mind was obviously playing tricks on me. I gave the letter to another inmate who was going to see him later that day, so she could give it to him. The next thing I knew I was being locked in solitary for it. I didn't know that writing a letter was against the rules. I'd written him letters before, and he thought it was cool. He said if it helped me pass my time, well, he was flattered.

As I discovered, correspondence with officers was a really big infraction to the Department of Corrections. They locked me in The Cage for three months. I was humiliated. Not only were my innermost thoughts read by correction officials, but the Department of Corrections gave my letters to the tabloids to embarrass me. (That shows just how low class and unprofessional the Department of Corrections was.) And of course, the tabloids referred to him as my prison guard lover and said that this was a steamy love letter. It couldn't have been more untrue. The letter was so innocent. I was obviously very lonely and troubled, and they were exploiting it.

They locked me in a room facing the Administration Building. I had a room that overlooked a staff bathroom in that building. I saw the correction officer I'd written to in there one day, and I talked to him from my window. I didn't know why he would want to hurt me. Why would he turn my letter over to his higher-ups in the chain of command? I thought he liked me.

He told me he was sorry. He told me the inmate I gave the letter to was a known "rat," and he panicked. He thought he was being set up, and all he could think about was losing his job.

Whether or not that was true, I have no idea. The whole embarrassing incident brought me back down to reality. I was in prison. I was not here to make new friends. My future and freedom became more important than a temporary emotional fix.

After ninety days I was released back into the general prison population. Prison officials structured the correction officer's schedule so that he was not permitted to work in any area of the prison where he could have contact with me. (The unbelievable and disturbing part about this was that the guards who I complained about raping and abusing me were still allowed to be with me.) This lasted about a year. I didn't see him much. I still liked him, and there were no hard feelings. Eventually prison officials let him resume his regular duties. I saw him more often, but it wasn't the same. I would talk to him, but I would never trust him again.

On the day I left Albion he showed up to say good-bye. I would miss him.

Months after I was home I was thinking about him. I decided to call him. I figured that since I was once again in the free world, the playing field was even. I wasn't looking for a romantic relationship. I just wanted to say hello. He freaked out when I called. He was frightened that he would lose his job if I talked to him. I realized that to him I was still a prisoner. I knew I had made a mistake.

Despite that one guard's "protection" of me for a period of time, day after day I was afraid for my life at Albion. I wasn't as much afraid that I was going to be killed by the inmates as I was afraid of the guards. I was powerless, and they forced me to have sex with them—at times violently—and there was always that fear of not knowing if or when it would happen again. There was no way to stop that at all. I was a target.

They would pull inmates' medical records to find out if they had diseases like AIDS, to see if they would be good sexual targets. They knew I was AIDS-free, so it made me even more desirable.

I think one of the most important things I want to clear up is that to the world for all these years it's been Amy Fisher the sexual person, the slut, the wild nymphomaniac. I was in prison for seven years. I was *raped* in prison—I never had consensual sexual relations. I never did anything sexual. I sat there reading books, doing my homework, or working my manual labor assignments. I got out of prison, and I dated briefly, like any other twenty-four-year-old. And then I got into a monogamous relationship, and we married. Except for that stupid brief time with Joey, I'm sure I've had a less promiscuous sex life than most women my age.

Chapter Nineteen

VIOLATED

I was raped numerous times in prison.

Once is too much.

If this happened in society, they would put these people, these animals, those rapists, in jail for years. But there, in prison, nothing happens to them. Also keep in mind that even if these incidents were consensual as the guards claimed—*which they were not*—it is still against the law.

Legally, prisoners are not in any position to give consent. Because of their opposing situations (guard and prisoner) and often extreme differences in size and strength (I was five-foot-three and weighed 100 pounds), the inmates' refusal, protest, or resistance would be futile or could result in harm to her or further retribution.

I was so naïve then. The guards would be nice to me, and I just wanted someone to be decent to me. I'd think, *This person is good to me, he cares about me*, and then all of a sudden he'd jump on top of me and force me to have sex. They raped me.

I was hysterical, always calling my lawyer, calling my mother, because nobody in authority at the prison believed me or cared.

My poor mother was so horrified, but she was always supportive. She'd cry, "What!? They did what to you!?" She'd then call the prison, and they'd tell her, "Your daughter, she has an active imagination. She's lying." And then it would get back to all the guards, and they'd say to me, "You're making problems for my buddy." They'd lock me in The Cage again.

That's why I got so upset when people would say, "Oh sure, she was raped in prison. She's a liar and a horrible person." Nobody can know what it was like. And the guards would actually go tell their friends, "I had sex with Amy Fisher." Even guards who never touched me would brag about having sex with me.

The guards who attacked me wouldn't tell their friends that they actually raped me. Guard pals of theirs would come to me and say, "I heard you gave so-and-so some." They weren't told that it was forcible rape. They would claim it was consensual. But even if it had been consensual, it was against the law, and it was rape.

But it was *never* consensual.

They knew they could get away with it because I was labeled a Lolita, a temptress. What better victim than a girl who was perceived as a nymphomaniac? Who in the world would believe her? The perfect target.

The guards would go around saying, "She's easy. She's wild. She's better than what they say in the movies." And of course, everyone would believe it because I was the Amy Fisher character they all knew from the media.

There were three incidents I recall the most vividly, mostly because of the violence associated with them.

The first of these was in October 1994. I had been in Albion for a year and a half. I had been locked in The Cage, which was in an old building with a stairwell that leads down to the basement. I had just had an attorney's visit, so I missed my recreation hour. Guard Gary DiSalvo was returning me to the recreation area. We were all alone because all the other inmates had returned to their dorms while I was at my attorney's visit. He closed the stairwell door behind me and just started sexually attacking me. He was vicious. I started screaming, but he ordered me to stop. He said, "Nobody can hear you."

He was a big fat thug who looked like Fred Flintstone. I wanted to throw up. I was wearing a dress, and he threw me up against a brick wall. He really hurt me. He had sex with me pinned up against the wall. I was screaming in pain, and he told me to shut up. When he was done, we left the stairwell and he slammed the door shut, locked it, and walked me back to my cell. He never said a word. I was terrified.

I thought it was an isolated incident by a maniac.

I complained to the Department of Corrections, and they said, "You have to prove it."

Well, what do you think he did? Do you think he gave me a semen sample in a specimen cup? Of course I couldn't prove it.

But I learned my lesson, and number two was a different story.

Bruce Kuttner was a correction officer. I'd make small talk with him, but he was often crude. He'd sometimes bluntly say, "I want to have sex with you." It was so casual, like him saying, "Hi. How are you doing?" I knew him for years. He had no class, and I never took him seriously.

The guards would just hang out in the housing area, keeping an eye on things. In July 1995, Kuttner was in the staff bathroom and called to me as I passed it. He pulled me inside and started kissing me and pulling off my clothes.

It was surreal. It was like I was having a terrible dream and looking down at myself. I couldn't believe it. I succumbed because I didn't know what else to do, but that does not make it consensual by any means.

It was rape, so there was no protection. I was like an inanimate object to him. It was terrible. He was always crude in everyday life, and this was no exception. I was smart enough this time, though, and I saved my underwear, which had his semen on it. The following week during visiting hours I wore that underwear over my own, and I walked into the bathroom and took it off and handed the underwear to my mother in the visiting room. She snuck it out in her pocket.

She could not believe that this was happening to me, and she could not believe how they handled it at Albion. When she reported something, they would say to her, "Your daughter's a prisoner. She's a liar."

But now we finally had proof.

And they still denied it!

So my mother spent thousands of dollars and sent it for DNA testing herself and then sued to get a blood sample from Kuttner.

After he was forced to give a blood sample, he took a leave of absence and left the state, probably thinking that if I had been lying about having the DNA, he would come back to work. But when the DNA results came back, naming him, he was fired. They didn't press charges against him. Just as it is Statutory Rape to have sex with someone under a certain age no matter what the circumstances, it is the same with sex between a guard and a prisoner: it is rape if a guard has sex with a prisoner under any conditions whatsoever.

To prison authorities, I was a mentally unstable temptress seducing their guards, and the poor defenseless dears just couldn't help themselves. It's amazing that I'm not out seducing all the men of Long Island now.

It took a while, but guards who I complained about during my time in Albion have since been convicted of similar crimes.

Today everyone is aware of these types of abuses. The rampant rape of female prisoners at Albion has since led to convictions of several guards. If you look up the court cases that have led to convictions or are now pending against Albion guards, you will find that many followed the same method that my attackers used and that the new plaintiffs' stories are disturbingly similar to my complaints starting back in 1994.

Ira Stiles was my housing unit officer for eight hours a day and he continuously tortured me, even though I constantly complained. Years later, in September 2001, well after I was released, he was charged with Third Degree Rape in connection with having sex with an inmate.

In 2003, with the help of the Legal Aid Prisoners' Rights Project, seventeen prisoners sued the New York State Department of Corrections in a civil case, charging numerous guards with rape in prisons throughout New York, including ten from Albion. One who was convicted was Sergeant Michael Galbreath, whom I had filed complaints about years before with prison authorities regarding his continued physical violence toward me; nothing had been done.

Back in June 2002, Galbreath had come to a plea agreement and was sentenced to forty-five days in jail and six years of probation for Second Degree Sexual Abuse and Official Misconduct in a separate criminal case. He was also required to register as a sex offender. What an insultingly low sentence.

Now Amnesty International tracks the sexual abuse of female prisoners at Albion and other prisons. But back then there was no such oversight, and I had no credibility. It was such a frightening situation to be in for a young person without anyone to help her, at the mercy of a system that was abusing her.

The third time I was raped was about nine months after the incident with Kuttner, in April 1996.

Dean "D. A." Schmidt was a correction officer who was always impossibly arrogant. One night he called me out from my housing unit. He called the CO in my unit to send me to the library. It was around 8:30 P.M., when the library was closing and all the other inmates were leaving. He said I needed to come receive "legal mail" from my lawyer, which was distributed at the library.

When I got there, he said, "Just wait by the desk." I did what he ordered me to do. He then went to the front door and let everyone out, and then locked the door. We were alone.

This experience was so horrible that I have tried not to think about it for many years.

He threw me up against the wall with my arms up and legs spread-eagled, like when cops search a suspect. I never saw what he did to me. I just felt the pain. He was so mean and brutal. I don't know if he used a condom or didn't. He was so vicious. I was just terrified.

This time I had no proof. Again nobody believed me. They let me report the rape, and even at that, they took the report three days later. They also did not use a rape kit, which could have proved my charge.

My mother consulted attorneys, who advised her to file a lawsuit, and even after the suit was filed, Schmidt still tortured and harassed me. I'd be eating dinner, and he'd get my attention and stick his tongue out and make lewd sexual gestures. He tormented me until I was released.

What better sexual target could these COs have than me? Who would believe that the Long Island Lolita didn't bring all this on herself, that she didn't seduce everyone with whom she came in contact? The swirl of lies was just overwhelming, ranging from inmates faking love letters from me that the media would reprint on their front pages without doing any kind of forensic investigation to find out whether they were real (they were not) to COs thinking they could get away with rape because no one would believe me. They were right. I bet that a majority of you reading this book who were around during that time recall those sensational and false headlines. And you believed them. How was I to fight that?

If you read the minutes of my hearing in my charges against the Department of Corrections, you'll see that although I had all sorts of factual proof, the hearing officials said I was "not a credible witness." They said my mother was "not a credible witness." However, "Lucky," the junkie inmate who turned against me to testify in exchange for a transfer to another prison to be with her girlfriend, was deemed "a credible witness."

Any objective person reading that hearing transcript would shake their head in disbelief. But that was what I was constantly up against. The New York Legal Aid Society Prisoners' Rights Project (which has brought the pending suit against the seventeen guards) claims that one of the biggest problems in New York's prison system is that the Department of Correctional Services does not take action to move these accused guards away from guarding women.

Since my hearing in 1996, it has been proven in court that this kind of intimidation and rape was occurring at Albion, as it does at any prison where males guard female prisoners. (That is the big problem here, and that *has* to change!) I can just imagine how many victims there are altogether. This kind of treatment of women prisoners was widespread among guards. I wasn't the only one. And it sometimes ends up tragically. There was one very pretty twenty-five-year-old prisoner, a friend of mine, who got pregnant by a guard and then died of an ectopic pregnancy.

In 2002 Dean Schmidt was convicted of Third-Degree Rape of an Albion prisoner whom he also impregnated.

When Schmidt, now known as inmate number 02B1536, was finally convicted and sentenced to one to three years in prison (he was denied parole in 2003), I felt like he wasn't put in jail for a long enough period of time. They should have put him away for life. However, his sentence mandated his release in July 2004.

It's so frustrating, because everything I said these guys did to me when I was in Albion, and nobody believed me, are the same things they were convicted for years later.

Do I feel vindicated? I don't. I am angry. Angry that I had to endure being so violated. Angry that the media essentially called me a liar and mocked the Long Island Lolita who fabricated stories about having sex with men. I'm angry that the Department of Corrections didn't take action and that other women were brutalized as a result. Even though the subsequent lawsuits vindicated me, as with Joey's rape conviction, it was too little too late.

I don't need society to say to me, "Okay, we believe you now." If every single person said, "We're sorry, we believe you now that we know the truth," it doesn't mean much to me to know those guys are still walking around living their lives with their wives and children and having happy times while the women they abused have to live with their horrific memories.

What difference does it make if people believe me now? Some of those sadistic rapists got away with it then, and others are getting off easy now. They took a young girl, who was in so much pain and so alone, viciously assaulted her, and then said, "Shh, don't tell anybody." It was awful. Then they would tell their buddies complete lies about me being so wild because they knew that, with all the exaggerated information about me already circulating, everyone would believe them and not me. I was destroyed.

In this instance I don't care about being right. I want these people to pay for what they did to me and others. And I do not want this to happen to any other new victims.

I did something very wrong, and I belonged in prison. But I did not deserve to be tortured.

Everyone always asks me if I'm angry at Joey. Well, no. Joey was a bad choice. My choice. I could have walked away any time. In prison these animals had me cornered. I was helpless. Joey, I've long forgotten. Those rapists and abusers I'll never be able to forget. They haunt me.

In 1996 I filed a suit in federal court in Buffalo against Albion, the guards and the Department of Corrections and also to seek relief to try to get moved to a federal prison, where I would be safer, because the state wasn't equipped to deal with me.

I was continuously harassed in prison, especially after filing my lawsuit. Typical of my treatment was the "smuggling" charge that was leveled against me. Sounds bad, right? It was plastered all over the media: Amy Fisher, wild woman and incorrigible inmate, charged with smuggling. Was it drugs like with almost everyone else? A weapon? No, not even close. I was accused of exchanging sneakers with my mother in the visiting room. An incredibly ridiculous, trumped-up charge.

The hearing was a kangaroo court. Remember Ira Stiles, the guard who I named in my lawsuit who has since been charged with the rape of another prisoner? Well, his wife, also a guard at Albion, was the witness against me. Remember, this was after I had brought charges against her husband.

The hearing for the shoe-smuggling infraction was on March 12, 1997, and it was a sham. They had no proof but it was the guard's word against mine and my mother's and photos that we supplied. They found me guilty, of course, and I was punished for ninety days. I asked for a stay on my punishment while my appeal was in progress and I was refused. Of course, after my three-month punishment ended, I won that appeal as I expected I would.

In April 1999, the Department of Corrections made a deal with my new lawyer, Bruce Barket. They hinted that if I dropped my rape case against them, I could get my parole hearing in May, five months earlier than I had been scheduled. I jumped at it because the deal I then had could have kept me in prison three more years, until February 2002.

This is what it came down to. Bruce asked me, "Do you want to prove your point and end up a martyr, or do you want to be free?" It was a no-brainer. The motion had originally been filed in federal court three years before. That's a long time to be tortured.

The Department of Corrections did protect me after that point in 1996. I was no longer raped or harassed. It was easier for the guards to prey on the next woman and not end up on *Hard Copy*. I had better living conditions. Strange, how they *suddenly* learned how to protect me. Basically I was safe. I never got locked up in The Cage after that. How did it happen that I suddenly went from being a troublemaking liar to becoming credible and invisible? They knew at this point that they would have to answer for their actions if they continued to harass me.

Chapter Twenty

THE BEGINNING OF
A NEW LIFE

Around the time of my federal suit against the Department of Corrections in 1996, I began to mature. Some of the older women would come to me and say, "Sweetie, just do what you have to do, don't fight everything." And I began to realize the wisdom of their words. Once the torture stopped, I had time to begin to work on bettering myself and my immediate world.

There was a committee in Albion called the Inmate Liaison Committee (ILC), which consisted of several inmates who represented the prison population. It was like a high school's student government. The population voted for a president, vice president, treasurer, and secretary. The committee met once a week to discuss problems occurring in the prison population. Mostly they met simply to discuss majority requests made by the population, such as staying up past 11:00 P.M. to watch the end of a World Series game.

They also met to see how creative they could be in getting the prison administration to consent to things that would improve the quality of life for the women.

To become part of the ILC hierarchy, there is a process. First each housing unit votes for an inmate in that unit to represent it. It is the job of that housing unit representative to bring problems, issues, and requests to the four ILC executive members at a weekly meeting.

When I was elected to represent my housing unit in early 1998, I was shocked. First, I felt that I didn't need the aggravation. My prison life was finally going smoothly. After five years there, the "Amy Fisher" novelty was wearing off. My 1996 lawsuit made prison officials do an about-face in how I was protected and treated. For the most part, by 1998 I was like any other inmate. I had no desire to be part of this ILC, which could potentially ruffle the feathers of the administration. I just wanted to serve my time and get out. I did want to fight for prisoners' rights, but I didn't want to annoy the powers that be.

What followed was like something out of *Analyze This*. I was told by some of the more intimidating inmates that I *would* do it. It would be *good* for me to do it.

I understood. I *would* do it, and I would be *happy* about it too! I figured all I had to do was bring their list of complaints to the ILC board and then I was done for the week. It didn't sound that hard.

After the representatives of the housing units are chosen, within several days those names are put on a list that is distributed to every inmate in the facility. The general inmate population then decides who from that list they want to represent them as president, vice president, secretary, and treasurer. The four chosen representatives have monthly meetings with prison administration, including the superintendent who runs the prison. The ILC term lasts six months.

To the dismay and shock of the prison officials, and to my own surprise, I was elected to be secretary of the ILC by my fellow inmates.

It wasn't that these women loved me so much. Actually, I'd say from the comments I heard on a regular basis that I really never fit in. I didn't mind, though; I had no plans to make Albion my permanent home. They elected me, they told me, because they thought I was smart, well spoken, and could do a good job of trying to get them some of the things they needed.

After the election, I was thinking, *Sorry, guys, I'm not doing it.*

As ILC secretary, I would have contact with prison administration. I thought I was going to be sick. I found out soon enough that the prison officials were feeling the same way.

I was going to step down when I started to think: Albion officials controlled everything I did there, and from my first day there they were unfair to me. They didn't let me pick my jobs like the other inmates did; they forced me to stay in housing units that were horrible; even if I earned privileges to leave those units, I was denied. I decided this ILC was the one thing they couldn't control. I was voted in, and I doubted that they wanted to tell two thousand women their votes didn't count.

I did vow to myself not to make waves during my time in the ILC. I planned to do the best job for the women that I could, but I wouldn't ask for anything ridiculous. I discovered early on, however, that the prison population didn't know what to ask for. They were so focused on requesting things like being able to stay up for a "late night" to watch a boxing match on HBO that they didn't realize that without increasing inmate revenue there would be no HBO to watch it on.

Although I was chosen to be ILC secretary, I ended up doing much of the work that was reserved for the treasurer. I took one look at the pitiful lack of funds available for amenities and decided we needed money. The Department of Corrections barely provided the basics.

I went to work immediately. I was instrumental in getting officials to allow toiletries and hygiene items to be sold through the prison. Before this, we were not permitted to receive these items, which helped boost the self-esteem of the inmates, from the outside world. Once they were allowed, the money generated from the sale of these items earned revenue for amenities that the state of New York did not provide, such as new TVs, cable service, and microwaves for the housing units.

Many people may feel that prisoners should not have anything. This is an easy opinion to have when you've never been there. Just being locked up is mentally draining. Being able to do things like watch TV helps prisoners pass the time and in essence minimizes the trouble they can cause. An inmate can even learn something by watching TV. By removing all forms of entertainment, inmates become more stressed.

After five years of manual labor, I finally had an office job half the day working as the ILC secretary. At least I now only had to mow lawns for four hours a day instead of eight.

There wasn't possibly enough typing to keep me busy for four hours a day, so I started invented things to do — little projects.

I wrote letters to all the cosmetic companies in the country requesting donations of hygiene and toiletry items such as soap, lotion, and shampoo that we could give to the women who didn't have anything. We thought it would be a nice gesture, and if we could get donations on a regular basis, it would cut down on the stealing, which resulted in fighting. I had plenty of time to type. Maybe we'd get lucky and get a few donations.

About a month later the executive team was called to the Administration Building. We were told that there were tons of boxes arriving addressed to us: boxes of toothbrushes, soaps, and lotions. The boxes kept coming.

We were admonished for not consulting prison officials before we sent out the letters and told that all of these donations would be returned. It seemed unfair. Many of these women needed these things and could not afford them.

Our ILC president caught up with the superintendent one day and asked her why the donations couldn't be distributed. The superintendent thought about it and finally decided we could give them out, but not just to women we thought were in need. We had to evenly distribute the contents to the entire population. For Mother's Day 1998, each inmate received enough hygiene products to last till the end of the year. Women were thanking us as though we had just given them new cars. I had never really thought about not having basic things in prison. I'd call my mom, and she always sent me what I asked for and then some.

We managed to increase earnings through the sale of things like popcorn, bags of candy, and nail polish. It doesn't sound like much, but it added up to a nice piece of change, which went into an ILC account for inmate prison items like microwaves and TVs. I also helped raise significant funds for indigent prisoners who had no money in their inmate accounts.

I was elected to a second term as ILC secretary. During this time I participated in a United Way video in which I spoke about the importance of education and how continued schooling would lead to more opportunities. I tried to explain that educational opportunities help people lead more productive lives.

By January 1999, both terms were up. An inmate was allowed to serve only two terms and then couldn't be elected again for a year. The women requested that I stay on. I didn't think it would matter because the rules stated that I couldn't. I was wrong. The prison administration allowed me to remain the ILC secretary. I was paroled four months later.

Chapter Twenty-One

A CHANGE IN PLANS

I had been in prison for two years when the change in New York governors occurred in 1994. Out went Mario Cuomo, and in came George Pataki. I barely knew who Cuomo was and definitely had no clue about Pataki, but, boy, would I figure him out in a hurry.

The newly elected Pataki seemed to go on an immediate mission to change the New York prison system. There would be an end to "violent" criminals participating in the work-release program two years before their initial parole-board hearing. That arrangement had allowed inmates to work in society during the day, spend several nights a week at home with their families, and spend the other nights in a halfway house. Pataki decided that the work-release program would be better suited to nonviolent felons. Somehow I can't see only drug dealers and addicts successfully maintaining nine-to-five employment. And the white-collar criminals like forgers and embezzlers, well, isn't that like putting a fox in a henhouse?

Because I had a five- to fifteen-year sentence, under the pre-Pataki arrangement I would have been eligible for parole after three years. Since I had already served time in the county jail, it would have actually been two years and a few months. But Pataki came in and changed all that.

When I heard about this, I was very upset and called Eric Naiburg. He said, "Look, the law's changed. We can't do anything about it. It's the law now." He continued, "You're going to have to grin and bear it another two years till the parole board meets." I had no choice.

I said, "All right," and I did that—I began biding my time.

At that point I'd already been in there three years. So it would be only another twenty-four months. I felt like since I had done all that time already, I could wait.

Eric assured me, "Be brave. It's only two more years, and you'll definitely be out. I have a letter from the prosecutor. The district attorney said you will be out."

The year was 1994, and I resigned myself to the reality that I would spend two additional years in hell. Apparently three years of torture and abuse wasn't a long enough period of time for me to be scared straight for my crime.

Two years later, though, I was prepared to leave my parole-board hearing saying, "Yes! I'm going home." My family thought I was coming home. This is what Eric Naiburg was telling all of us.

But the parole board told me I was not going home. By that time I already knew I wouldn't be paroled. Eric was to produce a letter he supposedly had from Fred Klein, stating something like, "We feel Amy should be released," and he never supplied it. My mother continuously asked for that letter and other documents he said he had, and Naiburg continuously had excuses. Finally, my mother said, "You know what? Maybe these things really don't exist. Maybe Eric's lying." I didn't want to face that. I thought Eric was terrific.

Chapter Twenty-Two

THE BIG LIE

To fully explain what happened to me in terms of Eric Naiburg's wrongdoings, I have to go back to 1992.

That fall, Eric sat down with me and explained that a plea bargain of five to fifteen years had been offered to me by the prosecution. To a teenager five years seems like a lifetime, and I felt like I would be getting more time than the minimum. I felt like if I said okay, I would be in prison forever. I said no to the offer.

Naiburg soon returned to me with a counter-offer and said that Assistant DA Fred Klein had agreed to write a letter recommending that I be entered into a work-release program after three years. Naiburg further stated that Klein would write a letter recommending parole.

My parents and I thought that a letter was a nice gesture, but not a guarantee. We felt it would be okay as long as it was documented in court during my upcoming sentencing. Naiburg explained that if the prosecutor recommended parole, it would be granted out of "professional courtesy." He further explained that because of the enormous publicity surrounding the case, the prosecutor would not agree to anything in open court. He figured after a few years the case would die down, the publicity would go away, and a letter would go unnoticed. I was okay with it. He was my lawyer. I trusted him.

Okay, on to 1997. Early that year I began my countdown to freedom. My parole date was August 28. The climate set by Pataki in the prison system was that *all* persons convicted of any crime remotely violent would not be granted parole and would rot in prison until their conditional release, or CR date, which was two-thirds of a prison sentence. For me that meant ten years in prison. That was frightening. It meant an inmate could follow all the prison rules, complete all the mandated programs, and do everything asked of her, only to be denied parole for the "nature of the crime." I wondered if I too would fall into this zero-tolerance category.

I shared my concerns with Eric. He reassured me that I had nothing to worry about. He said his letter from the district attorney's office was as good as the key to the front gate to freedom. In a few months prison would be a closed chapter in my life. He told me to start thinking about my future.

As my parole-board hearing was approaching I kept asking Eric if he had received the letter from the DA's office. I was calling him from prison constantly. This was my life, and I wanted it back. Naiburg had one excuse after another. He assured me that he had placed numerous calls to Klein and told me that Klein was busy, but promised the letter before June.

June came, and I was confused and upset. No letter meant no parole. My mother went to Naiburg's office demanding that he call Klein on the spot. She wanted to speak to Klein. She wanted that letter. The only reason I accepted the plea bargain in the first place was because of this letter.

Naiburg sweet-talked my mom, explaining that prosecutors were very busy and that he would go down to the DA's office and get the letter himself if necessary. Pacified for the moment, my mother went home. We would learn later on that Eric did go to the DA's office, but not to pick up the promised letter. He went to beg for one they had never even heard of before.

In June, right before I was scheduled to appear before the parole board, Naiburg sat down with my mother with some bad news. He informed her that Klein had reneged on writing the letter. There was nothing we could do because it was an "under the table" agreement that we couldn't prove. Naiburg expressed his outrage and condolences. He assumed that would be the end of the whole letter fiasco. But he underestimated my mother's drive to help me and to hold Fred Klein accountable for lying and reneging on an agreement and devastating our entire family with such a cruel promise.

It was no surprise when I was denied parole for "the nature of the offense." My parole hearing was a formality and a complete waste of tax dollars.

My mother made some calls in the legal community explaining what had transpired and asking what course of action would rectify what had happened. After almost a year she was pointed in the direction of Bruce Barket, a high-profile Garden City, Long Island, criminal defense attorney and former Nassau County prosecutor. Barket had a reputation for being honest and well respected.

As I wallowed in my misery and despair in prison, my mother met with Barket. She described the circumstances surrounding the letter and explained that I never would have pleaded guilty if there had been even the slightest possibility I would spend ten to fifteen years in prison. It wasn't that I didn't deserve to be held accountable for my actions, but that amount of time was extreme for someone my age charged with the crime with which I had been charged. There was no convicted seventeen-year-old in the entire New York State prison system who ever served that exorbitant amount of time for assault. Robert Chambers received the same sentence for murder.

Bruce looked further into the matter and found out what actually happened.

During this time it was like nothing went right. It really was like a bad movie. There was never a peaceful moment. It's kind of ironic, because my life is so quiet now.

In the summer of 1998 Bruce confronted me with letters I had received, and kept, from Eric Naiburg. These letters included personal statements and poems, which indicated that our relationship was more than client and lawyer.

I had met with Bruce on several occasions, but we never spoke much about Eric. Bruce was hired to file a lawsuit in Nassau County asking to have my plea bargain of five to fifteen years vacated because I had entered into the original plea agreement only after I was told by Eric that the DA's office promised I would be home in three years if I did. I did not hire Bruce to go after Eric Naiburg personally. In my mind Eric was still a good guy. It never once crossed my mind that he could have lied so deeply to me that it would affect my life, my freedom, and my future.

As Bruce started reading Eric's letters to me, I was livid. I had sent Eric's letters home to my mother over the years for safekeeping because they meant something to me. Eric meant something to me. I had no idea my mother would ever read the correspondence. I felt as though she had just read my diary. Now she had given Bruce my personal letters from Eric, and Bruce was reading them, analyzing every line as my embarrassment intensified. He was demanding to know what kind of relationship I had with my former attorney. I didn't know what to say. As a very moral and religious man, Bruce was shocked by Eric's conduct.

I admitted Eric and I were close. I wouldn't be specific with Bruce, though I didn't have to be—he had the letters. He knew how to read.

At first I had a very contentious relationship with Bruce. I had never had such a serious attorney before, one who wouldn't take my crap. He was a real authority figure, a former priest with high morals. He wouldn't stand for anything other than complete honesty and getting down to business. He was extremely disturbed by the inappropriate relationship I had with Eric. Bruce was all business and had a job to do.

Bruce was annoyed and frustrated. He flew all the way to Albion, and all I said was that I wouldn't talk about Eric. Bruce left Albion very, very angry with me.

I found it difficult to talk to Bruce at the beginning. Actually, the first few times I met him I didn't like him. I was used to calling the shots, and with this new attorney, well, he called the shots. I told my mother to fire him. She refused, saying that he was not hired to be my entertainer or my friend; he was hired to try to help me obtain my freedom. He was supposed to be one of the best, so he would remain.

A few days after Bruce left Albion frustrated with me, he sent Steve Kommar, another lawyer who was working on my case, to Albion to have me sign an affidavit about my relationship with Eric. Steve came to Albion, and I found him to be nice. He basically told me that Eric had lied to me and that if I truthfully described our relationship, no matter how embarrassing, there would be a great chance my original plea would be withdrawn and that in all likelihood, because I had already served half of my fifteen-year sentence, the district attorney would not retry me. He coddled me where Bruce did not. I was still immature, and being locked in a time capsule in prison did not help me mature as a person. By the time Steve left I had signed the affidavit.

When Bruce filed the lawsuit against Nassau County, there was a lot of publicity. The media went wild reprinting Eric's personal, innuendo-filled letters and poems. He denied all the charges against him in the press, but for a change, the law was on my side. Also, this time around there was no question of "here she goes making up stories again." The suggestive and inappropriate letters were there for everyone to see.

Dominic Barbara, the Buttafuocos' well-known attorney—he defended Jessica Hahn, the church secretary with whom televangelist Jim Bakker was having an affair, and he often appeared on *The Howard Stern Show*—disliked Eric Naiburg. He asked Bruce what he could do to help me. Bruce informed Mr. Barbara that having Mary Jo in our corner would really help. Mr. Barbara agreed and said he would speak to her. Apparently Mary Jo was receptive because she needed closure. Besides, she also hated Eric Naiburg because of the way he went after Joey.

In the early fall of 1998, Bruce and my mother met with Dominic Barbara and Mary Jo in Mr. Barbara's

Garden City office (which, ironically, is across the street from the *Long Island Press*, the paper I now write for).

According to Bruce, this meeting turned out to be a Naiburg roast. Surprisingly, Bruce and Mary Jo hit it off.

Bruce and Mary Jo began speaking on the phone after their first meeting. They discussed religion and spoke about forgiveness and healing. Bruce relayed my feelings of shame and remorse to Mary Jo. He also passed on a letter I wrote to her.

For many years I had wanted to tell Mary Jo how sorry I was. I realized how horrible my mind-set and actions were when I was a teenager. I knew words could not erase the damage I had inflicted, yet I felt I had to say something.

I would discuss my guilt, remorse, and shame with Eric Naiburg, who sympathized, but he had always told me Mary Jo would not be sympathetic. He believed that writing to her from prison would only create another wave of unwanted publicity and my apology would be misconstrued.

But in 1998 Eric was no longer guiding me, and I told Bruce Barket my feelings about wanting to write to Mary Jo to at least make an attempt to let her know how remorseful I truly was. Unlike Eric, Bruce thought it would be a nice gesture and one, in his opinion, that was long overdue.

I mailed the letter to Bruce, who then read it to Mary Jo over the phone. He told me later that day that she was moved to tears and relayed that she had waited seven years for me to apologize.

By this time I was truly starting to understand the enormity of what I had done to Mary Jo, and I was able to apologize and really feel it on the deepest level. It was no longer about being sorry because I got in trouble, being sorry because I was scared, or being sorry because I was in prison. I now saw more clearly that my immaturity and self-centeredness had almost taken her life. I almost left two small children without a mother. I left Mary Jo with a lifetime of pain. For the first time I was starting to truly comprehend the effect my actions had on her.

I had come a long way from the confused teen I was years earlier. There was a time right after the shooting when had I thought, *Okay, I'm sorry. Mary Jo is going to live, and the whole incident is over. Let's move on.* Unfortunately, I could not just chalk things up to a learning experience. It took me a long time to get that through my thick skull.

Mary Jo wrote me back a very nice letter as well.

Mary Jo was eager for Eric Naiburg to lose his license to practice law. If the district attorney acceded to my motion to vacate my plea based on inefficient assistance of counsel, that would mean they were conceding that Naiburg had lied to me about the existence of a private arrangement and might have to appear before the Bar Committee.

Bruce asked Mary Jo if she would write a letter to Nassau County District Attorney Denis Dillon, stating that she would not oppose my release if they decided that action was appropriate. In October 1998, Bruce met with Judge Ira Wexner, who was presiding over the case, in his chambers. Also present for the meeting were Fred Klein, who prosecuted me in 1992, Ray Perini, who was Eric Naiburg's attorney, and Steve Kommar. The goal, on both sides, was to keep the current motion that included Eric's letters private. The judge took it under advisement, and Prosecutor Klein said he would consider Bruce's request to vacate my plea.

During this time Bruce, who still had many friends in the Nassau County DA's office, was getting a lot of opinions and suggestions about the lawsuit he filed on my behalf. Some who worked in that office didn't feel I should be released and expressed that opinion to Bruce, who in turn informed them that he was now a defense attorney and that was what he did—defend people in legal predicaments and protect their rights.

Others who worked in the district attorney's office were telling him what would be needed for DA Dillon to accede to my motion. Apparently the DA wanted more proof than the word of Amy Fisher and her mother that Eric Naiburg lied to get me to accept a plea bargain. Were there any other attorneys or independent parties who had witnessed Eric making these promises? Bruce called my mother to inquire.

My mother told Bruce to call Christine Edwards Neumann, who was the original attorney hired to help me in 1992. She represented me for a few days then but was not a criminal attorney. She was the one who had recommended Eric to my parents. She remained as an attorney for my parents during my 1992 ordeal. She was present for almost every meeting with Eric. She was there when Eric told us about "the deal."

Phil Catapano, a prominent civil attorney with the Garden City law firm Monfort-Healey, was hired in the summer of 1992 to represent my parents and myself for any civil proceedings that would follow the criminal proceedings. He also was a witness to these promises.

By December 1998, Bruce's efforts to resolve the matter quietly to avoid any further publicity in the case were not coming to fruition. The motion was filed and the facts became public.

Bruce filed an initial motion in May 1998 alleging that the DA did not live up to the plea deal in regard to parole and work-release. The DA then filed papers absolutely denying the existence of the deal. That was the scenario we were working toward, and the position we believed was true—the DA refuting Eric's claims. The only question left for the courts was: who was lying—the DA or Eric? Of course we knew the answer. We thought Eric's inappropriate relationship with me was the motive for him to lie to me to get me to take the plea.

In the summer of 1998, the DA's office filed its opposition to the motion dealing with just the parole issue. In September 1998, Bruce gave everyone a "draft copy" of the reply, which contained the allegations about the relationship between Eric and me. In December 1998, Bruce filed the reply motion and released it publicly. The DA never filed an objection to the reply motion. They ultimately consented to that motion.

My relationship with Eric was sexually charged, but we never had sexual intercourse. Again, I was to blame for being so vulnerable, but he was my lawyer who was defending me in a case that had been sparked by an inappropriate relationship with another older man. In the clarity of hindsight, his behavior was truly reprehensible because I was never more vulnerable with anyone than with him. He was my lawyer, my protector, and, I thought, the man who would actually save me. He knew my problems. He knew my weaknesses. He read the psychiatrist's report after the shooting that said that I then had a "tendency to sexualize relationships with men."

Now looking back, I see that Eric's letters to me were very inappropriate. Twenty-five of them were included in the motion. In one, he sent me a photo of Madonna and wrote that she was "a beast compared to" me; he wrote to me saying, "You deserve a spanking, and I'm seriously considering it." He composed poems about me—*The New York Times* referred to Eric as being "besotted" with me in one poem—and he often wrote to me telling me how much he missed me. He signed his letters "125/93," which referred to the ages we would be when we got married. He told *Newsday*, "It was cutesy and playful and means nothing." One of many lessons I have learned from this ordeal: Attorney/client relationships are not supposed to be cutesy and playful.

On May 2, 1994, Eric wrote to me: "I stopped being your attorney a long time ago. I will forever be your best friend." What Bruce saw in these letters was that the relationship was more than "cutesy and playful." It was now clear that I did not have a lawyer who was capable of exercising independent judgment on my behalf. It appeared that he was motivated, at least in part, by a desire to conceal our relationship.

In February 1999, after months of phone conversations between Bruce and Mary Jo, she decided it was time to come to New York from her home in California to meet with both her attorney and mine to finally write down her feelings on the matter and forward them to the DA.

Bruce and Mr. Barbara decided to meet at a restaurant with Mary Jo. Bruce was unaware that Mary Jo was bringing Joey. Joey, in turn, brought his own attorney. Dinner went well. Mary Jo said she would compose her thoughts the next day.

Early the next morning Bruce received a phone call from Joey's new lawyer. He told Bruce that Mary Jo was on board but that there were just a few things she wanted in return. First, Joey and Mary Jo wanted to come to Albion to meet with me. Second, Joey wanted a letter from me stating that he never had sex with me, or any form of a relationship for that matter. He wanted me to say I made it all up.

I would have never met with Joey even if Bruce had said it was okay, even if it had meant my freedom. Meeting with Mary Jo was a different story. I would have. I spent seven years thinking about that.

This meeting, however, would never happen. Bruce knew I felt deeply horrible about what I had done, but he felt that if I said one thing wrong, or maybe if I just had a mannerism Mary Jo didn't like, she could walk out of the prison and say I was terrible, that I hadn't changed, and that I deserved to rot in there forever. Bruce wouldn't take that chance.

The second request was comical. Would anyone believe me if I suddenly said I never had a relationship with Joey? Of course not. It was out of the question. Bruce told Joey's lawyer these requests were not going to be considered. Bruce would not make a deal with the devil under any circumstances. If it meant Mary Jo would not support me, well, so be it. He would take his chances and mine in a court of law.

When Bruce hung up with Joey's lawyer, he called Mary Jo. Bruce told her he still needed her support. They had spent months talking about forgiveness, healing, and closure. Could it all have been a mockery promoting Joey's personal agenda? Bruce relayed the conversation he had just had with Joey's lawyer to Mary Jo. She said her agenda was not the same as Joey's lawyer's. She told Bruce that he had her support and that he should disregard the call.

Mary Jo wrote the letter in March 1999:

> I have come to the conclusion that Amy Fisher has spent enough time in jail as punishment for her crime. I know that at her sentencing I stated that I would like her to spend at least seven years in jail. She has now

been in for almost seven years. From my perspective, there is no reason to keep her in jail any longer. In fact, I believe that she should be released as soon as possible. I know that I am not the person who will decide when Amy is to be released. But I am the victim of her crime and I want you to know how I feel…

I can't help but feel sorry for Amy after hearing and seeing for myself how her former attorney, Eric Naiburg, conducted himself and encouraged an already sick individual to blatantly lie about issues in this case. She apparently thought she would be released in three to five years and that your office would recommend her release…

I had an opportunity, through the efforts of Mr. Barbara, to meet Amy's mother and to at least read letters Amy wrote to me and to write back to her. I am glad that both of these things happened…

It may seem odd that I have come to this conclusion. I know, however, that I am doing what is right for me and for my family. I have given the matter a great deal of thought and prayer. It is right and good that I can now say that I forgive Amy Fisher. It is a place I have only been able to reach through Grace. For that I am grateful. I hope that you will take into account my wishes when you decide how to proceed with this case.

Thank you for your time and consideration,

Very truly yours,

Mary Jo Buttafuoco

Once Bruce had Mary Jo's support in writing, he requested a meeting with DA Denis Dillon, and they finally met in late March 1999. Also attending were Mary Jo and Dominic Barbara. The meeting was very short. Since Bruce, Mr. Barbara, and Mary Jo were all in agreement, Dillon saw no reason to object. They determined that there was enough evidence to say Eric Naiburg, at the very least, acted inappropriately and my plea agreement was entered into under false pretenses. I had already served seven years of a five- to fifteen-year sentence. It was enough already. They would reduce my sentence so I would be paroled immediately.

A week before the new sentencing, around April 15, I was brought down to Nassau County Jail once again. I couldn't believe it: I was really going home. After all those years of hopelessness and despair, I would be free. I would be home by the summer. I would see my family again. I would be given the chance to live like a regular person. I would be free to show everyone that I was capable of leading a normal, productive life.

A court date was scheduled for April 22. But two days before, Judge Wexner sat in his chambers with Bruce Barket and Fred Klein, who was furious that the district attorney had agreed to this resentencing. The judge wanted to go over what was going to happen in his courtroom in two days. He was reviewing my file to make sure everything was in place. He started to read the probation report that was written in 1992 when Klein objected. That report was from 1992, and Klein wanted to know what I was doing in prison for the following seven years. He expressed concern that I could have been in possession of drugs or weapons or perhaps had even been violent. The possibilities were endless. The judge thought this was a valid point, and he excused himself, stating there was one way to find out—he was going to call Albion Prison himself.

Bruce felt sick. He knew that my first five years in Albion were an endless series of disciplinary citations. He was processing in his mind how he was going to minimize these to Judge Wexner. After all, my violations were for things such as not making my bed properly, dying my hair, and refusing to wash pots. It all sounded like a grade-B version of *Private Benjamin*. Would Judge Wexner quash the resentencing?

Ten minutes later the judge returned, and he informed Bruce and Fred Klein that the resentencing would move forward. Judge Wexner said he spoke to Aristedes Soto, my counselor in Albion, with whom he reviewed my file, and he determined that there were no serious disciplinary infractions and no infractions at all for more than two years. Mr. Soto concluded that I would do well when released from prison. Thanks, Mr. Soto!

But the tension didn't end there. Two days before I was supposed to be resentenced, the Columbine High School massacre occurred. The prosecutors were getting cold feet, which makes a lot of sense. One day two crazy Columbine kids go wild and the next day they let Amy Fisher out of prison.

But it all did work out. District Attorney Denis Dillon wrote his recommendation to the New York State Division of Parole on April 27, 1999: "As you already know, earlier this month my office consented to a motion by Ms. Fisher to vacate her judgment of conviction in the above-referenced case, because we concluded that the legal representation she received when she pled guilty in 1992 was constitutionally deficient."

Finally, there was a light at the end of the tunnel. They adjusted my sentence to three and a half to ten years. This time I knew I would be getting out.

When I went back up to Albion for the last time, I made sure I told everybody that it was just a rumor and that I was in fact not really getting out. I did that because even though the sentence was reduced, if there had been any problem they could have extended my sentence. A guard, an inmate, anyone could set me up. But I was about to be free.

Mary Jo, I almost took your life from you, yet you gave mine back to me. Thank you.

ABOVE: My former lawyer Eric Naiburg when he chartered a plane to visit me at Albion.

BELOW: My lawyer Bruce Barket in his office. (2000)

I'm having a large picture
made up of the best pictures of you
and me. I'm going to hang it in
my office so I can always keep
my life on you.

See you soon.

125/93

Eric

Portions of letters written by my former lawyer Eric Naiburg to me. Note the number above the signature.

Life after Amy is what
I feared ..... boring! There are
no phone calls in the middle of
the night, no hospital visits,
no worries that the world is
going to come down around my
ears, far fewer cameras and
a lot less fun .... certainly a
lot less fun. I miss you !!

When I get there you're
going to get the biggest hug
you can imagine —

Be good, be brave, be you

Eric

Chapter Twenty-Three

FREEDOM

The way they processed my release was by waiting until the night before and locking me in a room so nobody would do anything to me. Everyone was very worried about someone setting me up, trying to get me in a fight, or planting drugs in my cell, and then I'd lose my good time and not be released.

I remember sitting in the room, looking out the window that faced the front of the prison, and seeing all these cameras, all the media, and just about every network from every country. There must have been thousands of cameras out there from the night before, camping out, because the media knew I was getting out. And there I was watching them from my little cell. They could see me, but they had no idea who I was.

The night before I was released I was so excited. I was going to be free. The feeling wasn't even real. I just knew that I was going to be free. I didn't even know what to expect. I just wanted to get out.

I didn't know what I wanted to do first. But I did know that I didn't want to be where I was.

The next morning, May 10, 1999, I was supposed to get out at 7:00 A.M., but instead I watched all these other inmates who were being released that day. They were given their $40 and their bus ticket and a brusque good-bye—"Okay, bye-bye, inmate." But Amy Fisher was kept there, forced to stay in this little holding building until my mother and my attorney came to retrieve me. They were late. And I couldn't leave. I was screaming, "Let me out of here." I didn't want to be in there one minute longer than was mandated.

I was free, and they wouldn't let me out. I was being detained. I was flipping out. After seven years, I was flipping out.

They were worried about all the media. What was the media going to do? Kidnap me? All they wanted to do was take my picture. So let them take my picture, and let me out of this prison. But they wouldn't let me out. I didn't care about fighting the masses, I just wanted to be rid of this place. I'll go talk to CBS, I don't care. Maybe they'll buy me a bagel.

Finally my mother and Bruce walked in, and I began screaming at my mother. There was a lot of pent-up frustration. I walked out of that prison yelling at my mother and Bruce for being two hours late and leaving me in there. Bruce said, "Calm down, not in front of the cameras."

What preceded that, though, was a comedy of errors. Because they released me on such short notice, my mother had had no time to send me clothes to wear out of there, so she brought me clothes. What my mother was thinking, I don't know, but let me explain what she brought for me: a very tight polyester shirt that was so clingy you could see everything; a long, black tight Spandex skirt, and a padded push-up bra. She told me, "Well, I thought you'd want something nice with a wire after being in here with no wire for seven years."

So the first glimpse the media got of Amy Fisher now was in hooker gear. My mother swore that the outfit "didn't look so tight on the rack." She felt so bad.

When I walked out of the bathroom after changing from shorts and a T-shirt, Bruce, who was a former Jesuit priest, cried out, "Rose, what did you buy her? She can't walk out in this!" But there was no alternative. So in the photos of me leaving the prison you see Steve Kommar on one side and everyone else all around me in a tight circle so the media couldn't get a glimpse of my rear end in the Spandex. And Bruce and Steve were yelling at my mother, and my mother was explaining, "Well, I got her a medium." Of course, there were comments at the time that I picked my own attire. No, the fact is that my mom selected it and I had no choice. I couldn't walk out nude.

Amid the racket of all the reporters, film crews, and photographers, the prisoners were yelling out the windows, "Good luck, Amy."

When we left Albion, because there was so much media attention we couldn't even go to a local restaurant and get a decent meal.

The media were following us. The ten-car motorcade looked like a funeral procession for a president. It was a gigantic procession of cars and cameras to the airport, as if they were going to see something criminal occur between Albion and the airport. So Bruce said, "We can't stop to feed you." After seven years of Spam in a can, I still couldn't eat. I hadn't eaten since the night before because I was so excited, nervous, and anxious.

They hadn't booked a flight on a major airline because they thought it would be less conspicuous if we went on a smaller one. But what difference did it make if the cameramen were still sticking their obnoxious cameras through the fences at the airport? I should have just gone to Buffalo International, but I wasn't consulted.

They had a vending machine in the little airport we were at, and I spied candy bars and chips. I thought, *At least I'll eat something.* It was broken. So I got a Hawaiian Punch. That's all they had left and I guzzled it down.

I got on this small plane, and I was so nervous. So what did I do? I threw up on the plane. Because I had no food, I threw up Hawaiian Punch, and I was so upset because those little planes make me dizzy and sick. So they had to carry me into a car when we arrived on Long Island at McArthur Airport.

My mother couldn't drive me to her apartment because there were media people all over. She was living in Long Beach, on the South Shore of Long Island, and there were reporters and photographers staking out her building. So she drove me to my aunt's house and left me there. Now mind you, seven years before, my aunt didn't live there, she was single, and she didn't have any kids. Now she was married and had two kids in this house that was totally strange to me. Life had changed. I was lost.

All these relatives were coming over with their spouses and children to visit and say hi.

Who are these people? I've never seen them in my life, I thought.

It was very weird.

When my family attempted to figure out what to do with me, they realized that I couldn't go back to my mother's apartment because of the media people hanging around, so I just ended up staying in my aunt's house, where they didn't really have any room for me. I was treated well, but I felt like a stranger.

I was close with my aunt, but it was still peculiar living with her and her husband and her kids, who I didn't even know.

Everyone and everything was odd and different. I had been away seven years. Nothing was familiar. My mother had to leave me, and she was even living in a house that was unfamiliar to me. She had sold our old home.

Nobody I knew before lived in the same spot now, so even though I was back on Long Island, it was completely different. Seven years is a long time.

When I came back, I needed to go shopping. For my time in prison, I didn't have any clothes or many personal possessions. One day my mother picked me up and said she was bringing me to the Roosevelt Field Mall, which had been an unimpressive one-story mall when I left. We arrived at this upscale, gigantic, multistory mall, and I asked, "What is this? I want to go to Roosevelt Field."

My mom said, "Sweetie, this *is* Roosevelt Field." I disagreed: "No, it's not." She brought me inside, and I was terrified. It was so big and overwhelming. You'd have thought I was a toddler, because she was holding my hand, leading me around the mall, saying, "Sweetie, you wanna go in here? Sit down on the bench, and I'll pick out something for you."

It was terrifying being back in the real world. Everything was unfamiliar to me, but I was familiar to everyone. Everywhere I went people would recognize me. My picture was plastered everywhere. And at that time I still looked the same.

People would come up to me and say, "Amy. Hello. You're free," and all these women in the clothing stores were trying to dress me and take care of me. And I remember just standing there, thinking, *This isn't real.* I didn't know what to do with myself. I felt like I didn't belong anywhere. It was surreal. I felt all alone. Like being in solitary.

Everything was new. You forget what the most basic things are like. Even food.

And of course, there were all the technological changes. I remember seeing computers here and there when I was in high school. Some people did term papers on them.

I had never even heard of an "Internet." Everyone was trying to show me how to use the Web, and at first I couldn't grasp the concept. At the beginning I wondered, *What is this? What's the big deal?* Now I'm an Internet addict.

The best new discovery was the phone with caller ID. Also, everyone didn't have small cell phones like they do now, when I went to prison. They only had the big ones that rich men carried in their briefcases.

I wanted a cell phone very badly. I thought that it was pretty nifty to sit and talk to people wherever you were. My mother bought me one after I was home a month. I would call her all the time.

When I was nine years old, I broke my arm. I wore a cast for six weeks. Every day I begged my parents to take me to the doctor to have it removed. I was in agony. It was so itchy, and showering was a nightmare. Finally the day came for the cast to be sawed away. I was so excited, not only because the cast was coming off, but also because my parents had talked the doctor into removing it a week early, just in time for me to swim in a tournament I was looking forward to.

I'll never forget the doctor slicing through the plaster as though he were carving a roast beef at a family holiday dinner.

Finally he broke it in half, and I slid my arm away. My dry, red arm felt different. It was light as a feather and seemed to have a mind of its own.

The next day I lost the swimming tournament by a mile. My arm was weak, and I would have to work very hard to succeed at the next tournament.

Being released from prison was a lot like that experience—first trapped, then released, and finally striving to do better.

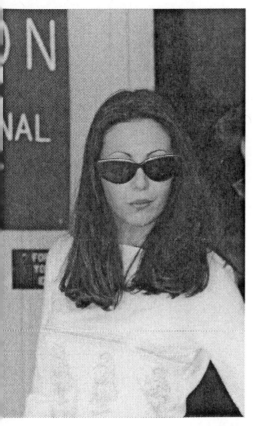

ABOVE:
Freedom: Leaving Albion Prison on May 10, 1999.

LEFT:
My mom and I on the plane on May 10, 1999, the day I was released from Albion.

TOP LEFT:
In a reflective mood on the plane coming home from Albion after being away for seven years.

TOP RIGHT:
May 11, 1999, enjoying my first full day of freedom at Jones Beach, on Long Island.

LEFT:
May 11, 1999, at Jones Beach, the day after I left Albion.

Chapter Twenty-Four

PAROLE

When I was released from prison, I was on parole until February 2003. For that whole period of time there was always that subtle reminder that I wasn't truly free. I had to meet with my parole officer once a week at the beginning, and toward the end once a month.

The first time we met, I received a very familiar lecture on how I was no better than anyone else and that I should expect no special treatment. After my seven-year experience, that kind of treatment was the furthest thing from my mind.

At the start, not only did I have to report to my parole officer once a week, but I was also subject to unannounced home visits.

When I was released in May, I had a 7:00 P.M. curfew. That following Fourth of July my whole family had a barbecue, and I had to sit all alone in my aunt's house. They felt so bad for me that my aunt ended up coming home early by herself. She left the party and came home and sat and watched TV with me.

The other rules included: consuming no drugs or alcohol, seeking and maintaining employment, staying away from drug zones, having no contact with Joey or Mary Jo, and consulting on any media invitation — the parole officers were like my agents.

Once I was blackmailed by a tabloid into talking to them, and since the parole office had never encountered anything like the Amy Fisher Media Phenomenon, they created special Amy Fisher rules to help me when it came to the press.

The Division of Parole turned out to be really decent. After about four months, I had my own apartment, I was attending college, and I was attempting to secure employment. They saw I was trying, and they got to see the real me, not the media caricature, so they became quite nice to me. They even moved my curfew to 11:00 P.M.

I had to go to their office in Hauppauge, Long Island. They'd ask, "How's everything? No drugs? No alcohol? No police contact?" It took about five minutes. Sometimes there would be a random drug test.

As time went on the questions would become more personal — about my love life, my family, my dog.

It was a welcome change from at first, when they were not that friendly. Like so many others, they initially fell prey to those misconceptions that were spewed by the press and they were somewhat tough on me. But I was confident enough to believe that since I'd been through this before and I was familiar with people's false impressions, if I was just honest with them they'd see me for who I am. And they did.

After a while they did get to know me. They began to realize: She's a decent girl. We like her. After six months, they really loosened up and were much kinder to me.

Chapter Twenty-Five

PIECING MY LIFE BACK TOGETHER

*T*his is the debut story I wrote for the Long Island Press *in June 2002. It best describes my life once I left prison in 1999 until I began work at the* Press.

PIECING MY LIFE BACK TOGETHER

There I was, sitting in class, proud of myself for trying to put my life together and become a benefit to society instead of a pariah. I was 24 and reinventing myself in college with a new name and a different look. It was great to be in this atmosphere, working toward my degree, among 18-year-olds who were on schedule with their lives. They didn't know who I was;

they were just kids back when my face was all over the news.

Every day I sat quietly in that classroom, hiding behind my Jackie O glasses, confident that I wouldn't be recognized. And then one day my English professor assigned the topic: write about an infamous Long Islander. I sat horrified. But weeks later, when the reports were given, I had to laugh ... many, of course, picked Amy Fisher. They all thought they knew me. Had me all figured out. They couldn't have been more wrong. I, on the other hand, chose Jessica Hahn. I got an A.

Let's go back to the beginning. I'm the first to admit it: I screwed up! I was a misguided, reckless 16-year-old who committed felony assault and landed in jail by age 17. That was 10 years ago. I've paid my dues, grown up, and have spent every day since trying to be "the perfect human being." I'm an adult now, thank heaven, and still can't figure out why I did what I did when I was younger, and why society thinks I'm a static cartoon character like Scooby-Doo, frozen in time, never changing.

To a large degree, I began the hardest journey of my life when I emerged from ball-and-chain-land three years ago. I thought I would simply shout, "Free at last!" and my adolescent mistakes would become a distant epilogue. I couldn't have been more wrong.

There I was, a financially depressed, uneducated young woman with a criminal record. I know, it sounds so awful. I decided to turn my life around. So when the tabloids and nudie magazines came calling, offering me big bucks, I turned them all down. Including *Playboy's* cool million. I said, "No thank you." I was going to take the high road, go to college, get a respectable job, and date decent men—in general, try to be "normal." It all sounds good, right? So now I'll fill you in on the reality.

In the deli, at the movies, at the mall, I don't mind people recognizing me. But it is at the workplace where I hit a brick wall. I discovered that Amy Fisher could not get a legitimate job. I was laughed out of interview after interview. They would think I was rich and applying for the job as a publicity stunt. They didn't understand that I was destitute.

Though hurt and dejected, I didn't panic. I came up with a solution: I would change my name. That would solve the problem, and I would be able to live anonymously like other people. It took about a month to legally change my name. Once this was accomplished, I immediately picked up the classifieds and started feverishly applying for jobs. People ask if I lied on my applications. I didn't. The applicant is asked if they've been convicted of a felony in the last seven years. I could truthfully answer that I had not.

It took about three days to become employed. I was now a receptionist for a computer software company. I was there a matter of hours when someone walked up to me and said, "You look like Amy Fisher." I smiled and politely replied, "I hear that all the time." I assumed that would be the end of it. I was wrong. The same thing happened over and over. Finally, I was summoned to the supervisor's office. She asked me if I was Amy Fisher. I denied it, but my words seemed to fall on deaf ears. I was fired, no further explanation, end of discussion.

Once again, I was living in dreamland, under the pretense that I could blend back into society unnoticed. I conveniently forgot that my face had been plastered on every periodical and television screen for the past seven years. I know, a simple oversight on my part. Once again, I stayed calm, took deep breaths, and tried to think of a solution. Okay, I got it—I'll dye my hair blond.

As I sat in the beauty salon, I became more confident each minute as I watched my auburn locks slowly transform into a pale shade of straw. When the process was complete, I felt like the liter of bleach made the difference. I'll admit, I looked a tad hookerish, but nevertheless, different.

With my newfound confidence, I spruced up my résumé and headed out to become a member of the working world. Once again I was hired in a matter of days, this time as a bookkeeper for an insurance agency. I was so excited, determined to work hard and do a great job. I loved working; it made me feel like I had the ability to do something positive.

Oh no, here we go again. I was being summoned to the supervisor's office after only two weeks. I walked into his office, trying to hide my paranoia. I barely had a chance to sit down when he blurted out, "I know you're Amy Fisher! You're fired!" He said that he didn't want the press showing up at his door. Did he really think I changed my name and appearance only to call the media to alert them of my whereabouts?

Whatever. I just left, determined not to let him get me down. There would be other jobs.

As the summer of '99 neared its end, I decided to go to college. Since I waited till the last minute, I had only one choice: Nassau Community College. I enrolled as a business major and was all set to start in the fall. During this time, I got another job, this time at a manufacturing plant, again as a bookkeeper.

My life seemed to be heading in the right direction for the first time in a while. I blended into college undetected. But I was terrified that someone would recognize me, that my anonymity would be blown and I wouldn't get to concentrate on my studies; or worse, that someone would call the press and I would have to drop out of school entirely. Thank heaven neither of these things occurred and I was able to obtain an education. I graduated with a business degree and a 3.5 average.

I wish I could say I was faring just as well on the job front. Unfortunately, I was about to relive the sickening experience of unemployment. My bookkeeping job lasted all of six weeks—a record achievement for me. This time the boss asked to speak to me privately. I assumed I was going to get the "I know you're Amy Fisher" speech again. To my surprise, the termination explanation had a new twist—my employer actually said to me simply that I had been "the topic of office gossip" and that some of my co-workers thought I "looked like Amy Fisher." She went on to explain how embarrassed she was, adding that she knew I was not Amy Fisher. However, my presence was just too distracting. I sat in her office for what seemed like an eternity, the whole time just thinking to myself how unfair this all was. I paid my debt to society; all I wanted was to work hard and earn my own way. I could save nuns from a burning building, and they still wouldn't give me a chance because of all the attention surrounding me.

As I headed for the parking lot, I kept thinking of all the money I wasted on hair dye. What was I going to do? I couldn't keep a job.

As the months turned into years, I was fired from job after job—ten in all. Eventually, I came to think of myself as a "temp." Even after graduating from college, it was the same thing—I'd be fired from a job for which I was completely capable, solely because of who I was and their fear of the press following me around.

I was becoming desperate. I decided to take a drastic approach to my unique dilemma: I would have plastic surgery.

After two years of living like a miser, I finally scrimped up enough money to have my face reconstructed. No, I'm not kidding. I needed to look like a different person, to essentially become a different person in order to be accepted back into society. Amy Fisher was a pariah; therefore, she could no longer exist.

Today I look in the mirror and sometimes don't recognize the person staring back at me. It's as if I have two identities, or maybe I have no identity at all. This makes me sad, and at times, isolated. In order to hide from the world, I was forced to hide from myself. To a large extent, I have to live a lie in order to blend in with society.

For the past six months, I've been able to maintain what most people would consider a good job at the same company. My co-workers have no idea of my true identity. This affords me the opportunity to earn a living, but not much else. When the girls go out to lunch, I eat alone. When they take a break to chitchat, I remain silent. I am terrified to strike up a conversation with a co-worker, much less attempt to form a friendship. I live every day with my secret, remaining in my own psychological prison.

There isn't a day that goes by that I don't wonder, *Is today the day I get fired?* Every time a newspaper prints an article about me or there is another "Amy Fisher biography" rerun on television, I agonize that someone will recognize me, and my financial security will once again be snatched away. I live each day not knowing what tomorrow will bring.

There are parts of my life that are very positive, though. I met a great guy and we got engaged. We have a 2-year-old son who is the most important thing in the world to me.

My fiancé and I want to buy a house so our child can have a backyard to play in and grow up like the rest of the children in suburbia, but how can we? Today's economy demands a two-income household to get ahead, and I can't secure long-term employment. My struggles are not only frustrating to me; they also have a deep impact on my innocent family. We have discussed moving away from Long Island, but this is not an option for us right now. My fiancé has his own business here so he can't pick up and leave, and I am on parole until February 2003, which dictates that I can't move away.

Sometimes I think my luck can't get any worse, but then something good will happen which makes me think of life as one big roller coaster. I've done wrong, but I have also been dealt some hard blows; granted, some were self-inflicted. But through it all I've learned to survive, learn, and grow as a person. To me, the glass will always remain half-full rather than half-empty. I know I will put the pieces of Amy Fisher back together. I have a positive attitude toward the future and remain with the hope that eventually I can be myself again, with acceptance.

Chapter Twenty-Six

MY MOM

To many people who followed the news of my story, my mother was a very sympathetic figure. At the beginning they saw her as a beleaguered mom attempting to help her daughter, but by the end they saw a stronger woman, an advocate for not only me but also other women in prison.

The phrase "life isn't fair" should be dedicated to my mother—a woman who never broke a rule in her entire life! Never smoked, drank, tried a drug while growing up in the turbulent '60s, or cheated on her husband. She worked six days a week to provide for me. She came home, cooked dinner, and cleaned the house. She would sit and do craftwork with me, especially on holidays like Halloween, when we'd make costumes together. When she had the time, she loved creating school projects with me. When she was younger, she attended the Fashion Institute of Technology to be a fashion designer. I like to think she passed her artistic talent on to me because I too enjoy artistic endeavors as well as fashion design.

My mother was liked and respected by her neighbors and clients at the store. That is, until May 19, 1992. That was the day she became the mother of the Long Island Lolita. After that, she was looked upon as the woman who let her child run wild. She was blamed for all of my mistakes.

That fateful week in May '92, my mother closed down her lucrative interior design business. For the next few years she tried to make sense of her life, of mine, of the future. She was going through the process of divorce after twenty years of marriage. She was being forced to sell her home, the last place I lived before prison. This meant she would no longer be able to sit on my bed in my old room, which she had kept exactly as I left it, and think, cry, and hope. Everyone was telling her to move on and get a new place, a new job, maybe even a new man. Sounded good, but all three would prove to be a challenge.

My mother decided she would buy a condo/co-op instead of a house the next time around. Living all by herself, she didn't need a lot of space anymore. Besides, it was the low-maintenance way to go. She had no idea that a board had to approve her application to buy into one of these developments. It wasn't enough that she could well afford the residence; in fact, she could have bought an entire floor of apartments for cash. It wasn't enough that she had perfect credit for her entire life. All these boards seemed to be concerned about was the fact that she was Amy Fisher's mother. A few of them actually asked her if she was planning on letting me stay with her when I came home from prison. It was as though I was a dreaded disease and the only way to prevent it was to not let my mom, the carrier, into their buildings. These boards also didn't want news trucks and paparazzi invading their quiet homes. So Mom was rejected from one posh residence after another. She packed up the family dog, put her belongings in storage, and moved into a single room in Grandma's house till she could figure out the next step.

Finally, after several months, a friend of a friend on a co-op board was able to get my mother into a building in Long Beach. It wasn't the greatest building, but it wasn't the worst either. It was acceptable and certainly better than living in Grandma's guest bedroom. Mom moved in without incident. She made friends with her neighbors, was quiet, and paid her maintenance dues on time.

During this time my mother, with her master's degree in hand, was trying to secure a job as a teacher. She wanted to help underprivileged children. She felt her passion for teaching and her compassion could make a difference in their young lives. She went from district to district only to be turned away each time. Her interviews always went well. She would leave feeling confident, but in the end she was never hired. She couldn't understand it. Mom went through her entire life being an overachiever—straight A's in high school and college, successful career. She looked good, and people had always liked her. It frustrated her not to be able to get a job teaching. After months of pounding the pavement, one of the interviewers let her in on a little secret. She wasn't being hired because she was Amy Fisher's mother. She was shocked, outraged, and ultimately disappointed. They basically insinuated that since her child turned out so terribly—if she couldn't teach her own child—well, how could she be expected to teach other people's children?

It's such a shame, because my mother is a very caring teacher. She applied in school districts where she would be paid a lot less than in more prosperous districts just so she could work with underprivileged children.

My mom was a substitute teacher for a while. Finally she realized that she would never be given the opportunity to make a difference, so she decided to go on to bigger and better things. She went back to college once again, this time for paralegal studies. If there were a profession that would embrace her it would be criminal law. How right she was!

My mother did a lot of legal footwork for my case and my suits against the prison. She was instrumental in my release.

There came a time when she had to start taking care of herself. I always heard dating in your early forties is as easy as dating in your early twenties. The abundance of forty-something divorced men in New York is staggering. But every time she'd meet a man, the minute he found out she was my mother, I was all he'd talk about. She'd think, *Hello? Do I have an identity?* It turned out one guy whom she dated just wanted to meet me. He used her and hurt her feelings.

A question I'm asked most frequently is: "How's your mother?" I am happy to say that today she is very active in her paralegal career, has a great social life, and loves being a grandma.

Excuse me for jumping ahead in time a bit, but I wanted to include a *Long Island Press* column I wrote about a special bonding time with my mother. This column ran the week of the massive East Coast blackout on August 14, 2003.

A BONDING BLACKOUT

Standing in my mother's kitchen, I watched the ever so bright high-hats above start to dim. Slowly the lights faded, illuminated, then faded again, finally cutting out altogether. Annoyed at the inconvenience, I grabbed a Diet Coke and made a quick exit for the backyard pool. I made a mental note to tell my mother to call an electrician to have her lights fixed. It never occurred to me that the power was down, or worse, that there was a blackout throughout the entire Eastern Seaboard.

I floated in the pool for hours, not a care in the world, oblivious to the chaos around me. It was so peaceful I should have known something was wrong. My cell phone that never stops ringing was silent. The dog wasn't getting zapped by the invisible electric pool fence, for once. I didn't even notice that the annoying buzz-hum sound the filter generates had ceased.

I also didn't realize that my mother was two hours late getting home from work. She arrived, frantically filling me in on the road conditions: no working traffic lights, the accidents, the inability to obtain gas. I was thinking, *What's the big deal?* It happens every summer, from people blasting their air conditioners; everything will be fixed shortly.

My mother begged me not to drive home. She started talking about the blackouts of '65 and '77. I had no idea what she was talking about. Power out for days? That doesn't happen anymore. We live in a high-tech society. Realizing a mother always worries no matter how old we get, I agreed to stay until the power was restored. It would only be a few hours at most. Little did I know I had just agreed to spend the night.

I had no idea what to do with myself. I couldn't gab on the phone, turn on the television, or surf the Web. I attempted to read by candlelight, but my rascally little son would have none of that. After several hours, the remnants of central air conditioning completely dissipated. My mother suggested we take a walk. A walk where? Oh well, I had nothing better to do.

It looked like one big block party—people relaxing on lawn chairs, children playing in front yards, having a blast. Don't these people have lives? How could anyone be smiling merrily during this horrible inconvenience? The heat was starting to get to me, turning me into the ultimate grump. I was cut off from the modern comforts I've grown to depend on.

As many times as I've driven through my mother's neighborhood, I don't think I've ever really seen it. I never realized just how pretty it was, with the flowerbeds so carefully manicured on the lawns and the mass of trees looming overhead. I guess one could say I was finally stopping to smell the roses.

That night when my son went to bed, for the first time since I was a little girl, I was one-on-one with my mother, with no distractions. I spend much time with my mom, but I realized we never really have any quiet time together.

We are either shopping or eating or watching a movie. We are always so busy making plans to do things in order to spend quality time together that we don't realize that all the activities leave little time for conversation. That night my mother and I talked and talked. I can't even remember half of what we talked about, but when the power was restored, I went home feeling more complete—and closer to my mother.

The blackout forced us to live as people did years ago in simpler times, a time when things like terrorism and weapons of mass destruction were not looming over us like a dark cloud; a time when modern menaces like drug addiction and divorce were rarities; a time when people were more laid back. I can't help but wonder if our lack of human communication is our downfall.

Chapter Twenty-Sevem

FINDING LOU

Being on parole was a strange experience. I was free, yet I had to follow the rules for a child. I had to be home by 11:00 P.M., the same curfew I had at thirteen. I wasn't allowed to consume alcoholic beverages, and I wasn't allowed to enter bars or clubs. I didn't drink, so that didn't matter, but not being allowed to be a part of a social scene was very tough for someone who was attempting to reconstruct a semblance of normalcy and rebuild a social life. The rules, as you can imagine, really put a damper on that social life.

The few times I decided to go out dancing with my friends I spent the entire time terrified that someone would recognize me and I'd end up in some tabloid and back in a jail cell for violating my parole. I stopped after three times, I was so scared. I never drank alcohol. I spent my time drinking Poland Spring water.

It's pretty hard to relax and have a good time under those circumstances, let alone build relationships. A girlfriend of mine suggested personal ads. My first thought was, *I'm not that desperate.* I thought that if someone had to literally take out an ad to get a date, well, how desirable could they possibly be? Did you ever read a personal ad? They all claim to be sincere and good-looking, financially well-off, and searching for their soulmate to cherish for life. Oh, and did I forget, most of them claim to be into things like hiking and biking, etc...What sounds too good to be true usually is: I decided to take a pass.

I went out a few times but never found anyone I wanted to be with on a regular basis. I dated a few guys I met through friends and, okay, one well-known TV newsman.

My same free-spirited girlfriend had moved from personal ads to Internet dating. I had only been on the Internet a handful of times and was still unsure how it worked. I didn't really see the big fascination with a computer and never bothered to get one.

My friend was a true girl of the times, and she rarely went anywhere without her laptop. I had yet to learn that the Internet was the key to the world. My girlfriend was playing around on her computer one day, and I was curious about what she was doing. I asked and she replied, "Oh, getting a date."

A date on a computer? Remember, I was not up on the times. As I hung over her shoulder I started to ask tons of questions to the point of annoyance. My friend finally told me to pull up a chair if I was so interested. I was, so I did. Little did I know that my first "Internet connection" would result in marriage, a child, a house, a dog, and a happy, secure life.

I had tight restrictions; it was difficult for me to be in social situations where I could meet people. So meeting someone online sounded like a good idea.

I met my soon-to-be fiancé (and now husband) through Match.com in the winter of 2000. I was using my new name. He said he was a millionaire. After numerous online chats, we met in person and we really hit it off.

One night I confided in him: "I have a confession to make before we go any further."

He said, "What?"

I answered, "I lied. I wasn't completely honest with you. I'm not exactly who you think I am. I'm Amy Fisher."

He responded, "I wasn't completely honest with you. I'm not really a millionaire."

When I told him I was Amy Fisher, he actually didn't believe me. He thought I was saying that to get his attention, the way he tried to impress me with his millions. When he finally realized I was serious, his response was, "Everyone has a past. I don't care."

We have been together ever since.

We got married on September 10, 2003.

Lou is a top-level videographer. He has a tough exterior, but a really soft heart. He is a genuinely nice person. He's the type of guy who stops to help stranded motorists even when he is already late for a preplanned event.

His ethnic background is exactly like mine—half-Jewish, half-Italian.

He's older than I am, but as young as I am in spirit. Some people say he and Joey are look-alikes, and he does kind of look like Joey, but that's where the similarity ends. Lou is honest and loyal. While Joey was out committing crimes, Lou, who was a New York City policeman, was walking the streets upholding law and order. Joey cheated on his wife every chance he got; Lou is a devoted family man.

Lou is sincere and dependable and has proven over the years to be my biggest supporter, my best friend. Besides that, he puts up with me.

No one really proposed. We had been engaged for about three years and just waited to take the final plunge. We talked about it a lot. But it was such a serious commitment to both of us that we took our time to make that final decision. Then suddenly we realized there was no reason to wait.

Since we decided spontaneously to get married within a week, my wedding dress was off-the-rack—simple, tasteful, and extremely uncomfortable.

We got married in Las Vegas in a civil ceremony. Most of our family members didn't even know we were doing it. The ceremony was so mushy; we were trying our best not to crack up. Lou saw that I was about to break up, so he began making funny faces to try to make me laugh. There was nothing serious about it. It was hysterical. Now I know why people rehearse for months.

Anyone can get married. Elizabeth Taylor managed to do it eight times. Britney Spears did it for a day. Marriage doesn't somehow make us more mature. It doesn't mean we're all grown up just because we say, "I do." It doesn't mean you suddenly have all the answers.

Lou and I dated for three years before finally saying those two commitment-filled words. We already had a child, a home, and an established life together. We always stopped just short of the altar for one reason or another. When two people live together and it doesn't work out, it is easy to go your separate ways. Marriage, on the other hand, legally binds you to the other person. Your finances become intertwined, and separation becomes much more complicated. You have to file for a divorce, divide assets, argue over alimony and child support. Before we jumped into something we might regret, we wanted to make sure marriage was the right move for us.

I have loved Lou since I met him, and I know he loves me. After three years we felt like we liked our life together and we were happy. I couldn't picture life without him there every day, and he said he felt the same way. So we made it official.

Somehow I thought that marriage would make me feel different, that I would feel more complete. The reality is I feel the same. Nothing really changed except my name. It's like when people ask you if you feel older on your birthday: you should, but you don't.

I feel like I married well. It is ironic because I never dated well. I married a man completely opposite of everyone I ever dated. My husband is honorable, works very hard, and is faithful. He doesn't have a regular nine-to-five job, so he is gone a lot of the time. Some women would complain about this, but I happen to like it. I do my own thing. I don't have to worry about cooking dinner (not that I am that good at it anyway), and I don't have to share the TV remote! I get to have the freedom of being single — not in the sense of dating but in the sense of doing whatever I want, whenever I want, and not having to feel bad that I'm not home. Of course, my son comes everywhere with me. We go visit friends and spend an exorbitant amount of time at my mother's house.

When my husband is home, he is really home. We do everything together. Even going to the deli is a family outing. My son loves this family time. He has learned that when Daddy is home we are going to do fun things.

Lou is a great husband and a great father. I can't imagine being without him.

TOP:
Lou and I in July 2003.

LEFT:
Lou and I in spring 2004, on a cruise.

RIGHT:
Lou and I on the spring 2004 cruise.

My Wedding, Sept 10, 2003

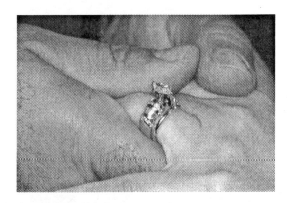

Chapter Twenty-Eight

BECOMING A MOM

A sk any mother what having a child is like, and she will probably start gushing about how it is the most wonderful experience. For me it was the first time in my life I loved someone more than I loved myself.

The concept of having a baby when you're in love sounds wildly romantic. Creating this being together sounds so intimate, so special. Of course, I learned in a hurry that that's when the "together" part ends. I gained fifty pounds, and my nose grew five times bigger! I was nauseous, hot, and dizzy all the time. Just when I thought I couldn't take it another day, thinking I would surely die, my doctor advised me, "It's time."

The whole experience in the hospital was bizarre and surreal. I had a scheduled C-section, and we had to pick up my mother, who wanted to be there with me. She was a nervous wreck and started getting paranoid. I had changed my name so that nobody knew who I was, but she started telling the security people I was Amy Fisher, to have them help protect me from the prying press. They created still another new name for me there and put me in a private room. But my mother was still telling everyone who I was. She meant well. She was doing it to try to help me, but I was so embarrassed. It was a wild scene.

I took one look at the six-inch needle that was about to enter my spine and changed my mind—I didn't need to have a baby. *I* was a baby. I wanted to go home. I whined and cried as the needle was plunged into my back. It would all be over soon. I would wake up the next morning my old thin healthy-feeling self with a cooing, smiling baby.

My husband, who can't watch *The Forensic Files* without wincing, actually watched my entire C-section procedure as if he were a curious med student. Being in a drug-induced haze, I don't remember much. A little pressure, my husband announcing, "It's a boy!" like it was a big surprise after three sonograms. As I lay lifeless, my joy-filled husband had the entire operation room staff posing for pictures.

Brett was born February 22, 2001.

After three days in the hospital, I was desperate to go home. I took out my pre-baby stretch jeans excited at the prospect of seeing my old self again. I managed to pull one pant leg to around mid-thigh when I realized they weren't going any higher. I panicked! I was still gigantic and would probably end up leaving the hospital in a nightgown because I had nothing to wear. I called my husband in a frenzy. He said he would get me something.

In typical male fashion, he called my mother, explained the problem, and told her to get me clothes immediately. Remember the last time she did that for me, what a disaster that turned out to be? This time, instead of Spandex and a tight blouse, my mother ran to K-Mart and bought a large sweat suit in the men's section.

When we were finally leaving the hospital, we were quite a sight in the parking lot. There I was in K-Mart men's sweats with a screaming infant and a husband cursing as he realized the car seat he purchased wasn't as easy to install as it had looked on the box. Perhaps he should have saved the instruction manual. So this was the American Dream.

Brett's birth was marred by the press for a fleeting moment. In January 1999, someone tipped off the sleazy tabloid the *Globe* that I was pregnant. They gave the paper one of those "anonymous" stories for which people get paid. My private moment was invaded. Right after Brett was born, the *Globe* kept calling my home, saying they were doing a story on his birth, and did we want to be interviewed? By the *Globe*? No, thanks anyway.

They pointed out that they knew where I lived and would get a photo of my newborn whether I approved or not, and that if I didn't cooperate, well, the story would read in typical tabloid form. I was so upset. It was a beautiful experience for me. I didn't want it ruined with ugly tabloid tales. Lou and I agreed to sit down and tell them how happy we were, let them take a family photo, and in return I got them to not run the story with an inflammatory headline like "Lolita Gives Birth." It turned out not to be so bad for a tabloid story, and they went away as quickly as they had arrived. But that's my life, even to this day.

I've had three-plus years to adapt to motherhood and family life. What started out as an overwhelming experience has turned into the most wonderful one. And now we're about to repeat the process. Our second bundle of joy will arrive in March 2005, and we are so excited we can hardly stand it.

When Brett was two years old, he needed surgery. I went for several medical opinions, hoping someone would say he didn't need an operation. No such luck. I think his operation was harder on me than on him. I held him down as he was put to sleep. He kicked, fought, and finally went limp. I pulled his favorite "blue blankie" from his grasp and was forced to leave the room.

The procedure was supposed to last two hours, so after two hours on the dot I ran to the front desk asking to see my little boy. I was told he was still in surgery. Two hours turned into three hours, then four. I was hysterical. I was thinking the worst possible thoughts. Finally, when I thought I was about to lose my mind, I was told I could see him.

Seeing your child in pain and being helpless is the worst. Worse than being arrested, worse than prison, worse than anything that I had ever experienced.

I can't be objective about Brett. He's a perfect child. He's smart and cute. He loves Thomas the Tank Engine, Bob the Builder, Spider-Man, and SpongeBob. He loves his seventeen-year-old half-brother Frank, who lives with us, and his new puppy, Fuzzy.

This was the first year he went to summer camp, although his backyard is like a summer camp. He is overly indulged by his grandmother (any surprise?), and, okay, his parents too.

Lou plays in baseball leagues at night, and Brett gets out his T-ball so he can "practice to be on Daddy's team."

I look at him now scampering around the house wearing his goggles, tool belt, and, in the summer, SpongeBob winter boots, and I can't believe how special he is and how well my life has turned out. In my darkest days—and there have been many—I never would have dreamed that I would make it to this place.

I have decided I'm not going to share stories about my past mistakes with my son until he starts to ask questions. I think it would be like when I was ten and my mother started talking to me about the birds and the bees. I remember thinking, *Why is she telling me this stuff?* I don't want to initiate a serious talk with my son before he is ready, only for him to wonder why I am telling it to him.

My eight-year-old cousin, who knows me only by my new name, recently asked me what prison was like. The question flew at me with the speed of a major-league fastball. I was driving the car, and I almost crashed.

I was told I am her idol. She says she wants to be like me when she grows up, and I think, *That poor kid, she doesn't know.*

My mind was spinning when she asked that question. I was thinking at lightning speed what to tell her. What had she heard, how much did she know, where did she hear it, and would it change the affection she felt for me?

I simply asked, "Why are you asking me?"

She gave me a typical kid answer: "I don't know, I just am."

I remained silent, not knowing what to say. She waited and said, "So what's it like?"

I decided to give her the generic version. "I think," I said, "that prisoners wear uniforms and have lots of rules, like a strict bedtime and specific times they eat their meals." She was trying to keep the conversation going.

"So what kind of food do they eat in prison?" I thought, *Oh, an easy one.* I rattled off about macaroni and cheese and tuna sandwiches. I was able to change the topic so she had a tough time initiating it again. I outsmarted an eight-year-old, but soon she will be nine, then ten, and so on. I figured out that she had heard something, but I was too much of a coward to find out what. I'm praying next time she'll just ask her mother.

When Brett has these questions, I won't be able to change the topic and pray that next time he will ask someone else. I'll have to face my mistakes and explain them to my child. I make sure to always teach him about what is right and what is wrong. And I think he'll understand and be understanding. I will explain to my son that we all make mistakes, but we should learn from them and not repeat them.

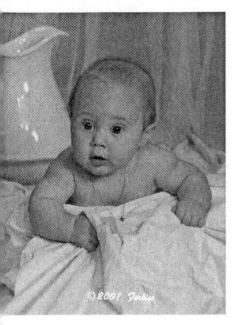

TOP LEFT:
My son Brett at 5 months old.

ABOVE: Brett (2004)

BELOW: Brett (2004)

ABOVE: Brett in our backyard. (2004)

ABOVE:
Brett and I having a deep
discussion. (2004)

ABOVE: At home with Lou, Brett, Me, and Frank.

Chapter Twenty-Nine

GETTING A JOB

In 2002 I was working in the business sector. I had a job that I hated, but I was constantly afraid I'd be fired from it. There wasn't a day that went by that I didn't worry about my financial security because of my infamous past.

Being an educated, creative woman in my late twenties, I hoped for a career I would enjoy. But I also yearned for public acceptance. I had come a long way from the sixteen-year-old girl who made worldwide news with one regrettable and indefensible act.

I knew I wanted something other than the job I had, which was just a source of money, not personal fulfillment. I had no idea what I would enjoy doing—or who would hire me to do it even if I figured it out.

As fate would have it, I received a call from my lawyer, Bruce Barket, informing me that a new upstart Long Island newspaper was launching its first issue and wanted me to write an article for them.

My immediate reaction was a firm "no!" If I turned down shows like *Dateline* and *Primetime Live*, what made him think I would want to write something for what I thought was a little community paper? Boy, was I off base. The paper is one of the top ten weeklies in the country, and it's still growing.

I was struggling from one job to the next, paycheck to paycheck, with an uncertain future, yet I was not willing to give up my anonymity. I was determined to succeed without using my notoriety.

After several months and many refusals, Bruce convinced me to meet with representatives from the persistent paper. We had a very nice dinner where I met Robbie Woliver, the editor in chief, and Bill Jensen, the managing editor. Bruce was also there. Robbie and Bill asked if I would write an article for them, and they agreed that I would not have to run a recent photo of myself with it. I was concerned about outing myself and losing the job I currently had. Bruce encouraged me to write the article, thinking it would help me to tell Long Islanders what I was going through and how my life was going.

I liked Robbie and Bill and trusted them, but I was inclined to dismiss their offer. After all, being in the public eye had never allowed me to live a normal private life. Why would I purposely put myself out there again?

After much thought, I realized that hiding under a rock hadn't allowed me to be anonymous. There was always someone there to turn over that rock. Why not let everyone know what my life was really like?

The biggest misconceptions about Amy Fisher were that I was wealthy and led a glamorous life, that I was heartless and cold, and that I remained that teenage seductress everyone remembered from the news. Wrong. Although I was plastered like wallpaper all over the media, I did not become rich; in fact, I was quite destitute. I lead a very ordinary life. And I am obviously no longer a teenager. I figured I'd write the story and clear up those and many other misconceptions. I suggested that I update my life for a cover story.

The first article I wrote, "Piecing My Life Back Together," generated a lot of positive attention. I received hundreds of thousands of letters from the public and the media around the world. It appeared that people were interested in what I had to say. I met the publisher, Jed Morey, who was incredibly supportive and generous to me, and I grew to trust them at the paper more and more each day. I was asked to do several follow-up articles for the publication, which began as the *New Island Ear*.

I started writing articles as a freelancer. I discovered I really enjoyed it. Writing was a therapeutic outlet. I figured it would be fun while it lasted, but I didn't quit my day job. I mean, I didn't think of myself as a professional writer; after all, I went to college for business, not journalism (although I took and aced many writing courses). I assumed it was a flash-in-the-pan event that would leave my life as quickly as it had entered it.

I was soon surprised when a major New York daily offered me a job as a columnist for an extremely generous salary. I was so excited that I almost said yes. After giving it some serious consideration, I declined the offer. After all, this was the same newspaper that had called me nothing less than "trash" for the past ten years; now they wanted me on their staff.

I decided to stay with the people who gave me a break when no one else would—the people who were perceptive enough to see me as a person and to take a chance on giving me a second chance. After a short while the *Ear* evolved into the *Long Island Press*, an award-winning weekly newspaper that is giving its local competitor, *Newsday* (a daily that had a field day with my original story), quite a run for its money. I was thrilled that my first story grew into a weekly column. I had found a new home.

I have discovered I have a knack for writing human-interest stories, many inspired by the letters I receive and some inspired by current events. I also enjoy sharing my own personal experiences, and I have been very pleased by all the mail from readers saying that they find it inspirational in some way. Currently I'm covering the true-crime beat.

I write at home, at my computer. I do most of my research from home, and I am assisted at the *Press* by a talented, young editorial assistant, Tim Bolger. Sometimes I go to the *Press* office to meet with Robbie or conduct a special interview, such as I did by phone with best-selling crime writer James Patterson or in person with *Survivor*'s Rob Cesternino.

I take the job very seriously. My work is always in on time. And I have come to love writing. It is a very fulfilling part of my life. I feel like the people I work with are my friends, and the feedback I receive from readers is incredibly fulfilling.

After struggling to establish a career for several years, I have one. It's ironic that I despised the media for how they treated me and now I'm one of them.

I've also always had an artistic side, and I've pursued that as well. When my son was born, I received a lot of personalized presents—picture frames, photo albums, piggy banks, etc., with his name on them, or hand-painted one-of-a-kind items. I absolutely loved getting these gifts.

In between feedings and diaper changes, I had quite a bit of time on my hands. I was used to working, not sitting around watching daytime soaps. I was bored. My husband suggested I find a hobby. He suggested things like needlepoint. Needlepoint? Yes, he was serious. He told me his mother would help me get started. I passed on the needlepoint bonding, as I don't feel I'm really the needlepointing type.

I decided to decorate my son's room instead. I figured that would keep my attention till I could go back to work. I was going to make my son his first table and chair set. I figured I could finish it by the time he was ready to actually use it. I purchased an unfinished set of wooden chairs and a table, primed them, and decided to paint a few animals on them. The project I thought would take months took only a week, and the few animals I planned on painting turned out to be an entire jungle. I polyurethaned my creation and decided it was pretty good. I went out and bought an unfinished wood toy chest, rocking chair, and step stool and painted my jungle on them too.

When I finished my projects, my son's room looked like it belonged in a home décor magazine. The project alleviated my boredom, satisfied my creative side, my son had a great room, and it was time for me to go back to work at a real job.

As my friends began coming to my home, they would notice the room accessories I had painted, comment on how terrific they thought the furniture was, and then, without fail, ask where I had purchased them. I explained that they were the one-of-a-kind results of my boredom.

People were asking how much I would charge to paint these items for them. I wasn't in the children's decorative business. I had no idea. Besides, how could I charge my friends, and now that I was planning on returning to work, where would I find the time to paint?

I relented and painted a toy chest for one of my girlfriends. Someone she knew saw hers and just had to have one. She called me and told me to decide how much I was going to charge for them because people really wanted to buy them. So I started painting children's furniture in my spare time.

I started a business, advertised it, put it on the Internet, and began to sell lots of items. I made a firm decision to not associate my name with it. I knew that I would sell much more from my notoriety, but I wanted to do this on its own merits. And it was a success.

Once I started writing my weekly column for the *Long Island Press*, I gradually stopped painting furniture. Every once in a while I paint a piece for someone I know, but I just don't have the time to paint on a regular basis.

I'm about to enter the broadcasting world as co-host of a new live morning show on 98.5 The Bone (WBON-FM), a classic rock radio station on Long Island. For me, it will be the radio version of my column.

Another exciting venture is writing books. Through my column at the *Long Island Press* I have been asked by the legal representatives or families of several high-profile prisoners to write books about them and investigate their cases. I love researching and writing about true crime, and I'm a passionate reader of both fiction and nonfiction crime books. I think I've had the kind of unique experience that would allow me to do a great job with this. I've already begun research on a remarkable real-life mystery.

ABOVE:
At home, working on my column.

BELOW:
My publisher, Jed Morey.

Some of my cover stories and columns for the *Long Island Press* and the *New Island Ear*. (the *Press'* original name)

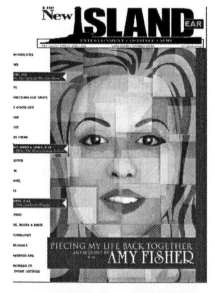

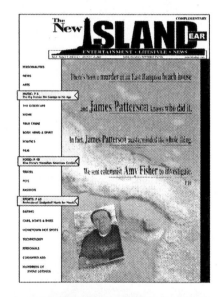

Chapter Thirty

REVISITING JOEY

This is the cover story I wrote for the *Press* when Joey was charged with insurance fraud on December 17, 2003, in California. It was the first time I talked about him in public.

When I first heard that Joey Buttafuoco was being charged with Statutory Rape in 1993, I was somewhat relieved.

Well finally, they're going to do something, I thought. I knew the authorities believed me by this time. They said that they believed me almost from the beginning.

But at the time, they figured it was too painful for Mary Jo and they were going to drop it. And they figured I was just a crazy kid and they didn't want to deal with the whole fiasco. They wanted it to go away. They were sick of the media.

But then when Joey was running around saying, "I didn't do it," all over national television. They finally got so sick of him, they said, "Let's just indict him and throw him in jail for a little while, teach him a lesson." I was thinking, *It's about time.*

I thought that they'd actually put him in jail for a substantial amount of time. They gave him six months for Statutory Rape. It's not right.

OLD DOG, SAME TRICKS

Several weeks ago, I was getting ready to attend my mother's birthday party when I received a call from one of my best friends. She was in the hospital, having just given birth.

"How wonderful," I told her, knowing the joy she was experiencing. I thought she had called to tell me about the baby.

Nope, she just had to call to tell me Joey Buttafuoco was arrested … again! I quickly laughed, not really surprised that he would be in trouble with the law.

I would have rather discussed the baby. I keep hoping I can separate our lives, but I can't.

That night, every news station covered Buttafuoco's arrest for insurance fraud, and many newspapers followed suit the next day. The headlines did not scream, "Convicted sex offender, probation violator, wannabe actor arrested for the third time in a decade!" Nah, there's no fun in that. Instead, every story started off explaining how he made headlines years ago when his teenage girlfriend shot his wife. Most of the articles never even bothered to describe his past troubles with the law.

I have spent 12 years futilely attempting to distance myself from Joey Buttafuoco, as one might try to get rid of psoriasis. Just hearing his name makes me nauseous. I'm the wild child who grew up. To a teenager, which is what I was when I met him, Joey Buttafuoco was right up there with X-rated movies, violent video games, and getting drunk: a taboo we outgrow and eventually prefer to forget. We all have sections of our lives we'd rather keep to ourselves for fear of disapproval from peers, family, and friends. I keep trying to throw my skeleton back in the closet, but he is forever jumping out to star in B-movies, perp walks, and mug shots.

The tabloid '90s enabled Buttafuoco to cash in on his notoriety. He took advantage of the millions to be made. He wanted to become a movie star, believing he was famous instead of realizing he was just infamous.

He left Long Island with the dream of being an actor and hobnobbing with the rich and famous. Before Jessica Simpson and Paris Hilton, there was Joey Buttafuoco, pursuing his dream in such unheard-of films as *Better Than Ever* and *The Underground Comedy Movie*. His résumé? Having sex with a minor and incarceration for statutory rape; soliciting a prostitute in California; probation violation and more jail time. I guess having been on television on both coasts for these offenses, he felt ready for the big screen.

Joey Buttafuoco essentially is the boy who never grew up, a lawbreaker who lives in his own world of "anything goes." He doesn't adhere to the spoken or unspoken rules of society, and when caught, the consequences for him have been minimal. I spent seven years in prison for my horrible act and four years on strict parole, and I learned my lesson. I learned why I did it, and I learned I must pay society and my victim back by being a good person. What he talked me into doing was unthinkable, and although I was a mixed-up kid at the time, I take responsibility for my actions and try to live a respectable life.

But it's different for Joey Buttafuoco. The slaps on his wrists didn't teach him anything. Perhaps that's why he never changes his behavior. Buttafuoco has been involved in illegal activities in the auto repair business for years. I was witness to many. But a decade ago, the authorities in New York didn't care. My lawyer went to the police about Buttafuoco's unsavory business practices, but they did nothing. The authorities in California and the federal government seemed to do the homework the Long Island authorities let slide. Unbelievably, Joey still is doing the same thing now. His most recent arrest could land him in prison for up to six years. It will be interesting to see if his luck has finally run out.

Joey Buttafuoco had to sit in the L.A. County lockup, initially unable to post his $50,000 bail. It's almost comical that after the millions he made from the tabloids being the

"Long Island Lothario," facing off on *Celebrity Boxing* (his match against the woman ex-wrestler Chyna was a low point of his "career"), his acting career, and his illegal auto body shop activities, he couldn't come up with the bail money.

When I first got out on parole, Joey Buttafuoco told reporters, "You haven't heard the last of Amy Fisher," insinuating I would at some point get in trouble again. I went back to school and earned my degree. I am married. I have a child. I have a career. I am working on causes to help troubled teens and to keep guns out of the hands of kids—things that will make society better. Sorry, Joey, you got it all wrong. Again.

Since this story ran, Joey has been sentenced to one year and is currently serving time in jail.

Chapter Thirty-One

HOW I CAN MAKE A DIFFERENCE

There have been several causes I considered getting involved with to help make a positive difference in other people's lives. One is keeping guns away from minors. As with my experience, too many young children are being injured or killed, or have injured or killed someone else, because of easy access to guns. The more I thought about it and talked to people in the field, I realized the best way to get a gun-safety message across was by talking about my experience and offering my help to gun-control organizations, whether through speeches to young people, public service announcements, or ads.

I also wanted to work to help girls who are at risk and families caught in a cycle of abuse. I am a survivor of an abusive home, and it is something that definitely turned me in the direction I took as a teenager. I realized once again that I could do the same sort of outreach on this issue as with gun control. I am at the service of any legitimate organization that needs me.

But as I was writing this book, one thing kept coming back and haunting me, and that was how women are tortured in prison. I spent many a night researching until four in the morning, devouring every article and news item that I could find, reading up on the state of women in prison. It is an embarrassment and, very often, a crime. Women are harassed, abused, molested, and raped in prison, and for many there is no recourse. Uneducated women are sent to prison supposedly to be rehabilitated, and they are just warehoused. It is unacceptable that poor women are sent far away from their kids and that there is no money to have the children take the long trip to see their moms. As I mentioned in an earlier chapter, things are so bad that organizations such as Amnesty International, which is known for tracking prison torture in countries like Rwanda and Iraq, are now tracking conditions in American women's prisons.

Many prisoners are denied their basic rights and suffer everything from the refusal of medical treatment to the kind of physical abuse I suffered. Unfortunately, funding for legal services for abused prisoners has been cut all across America. The Legal Aid Society Prisoners' Rights Project (they help indigent women and bring class action suits) and the Amnesty International prison projects are some of the very few groups striving to end this inhumane treatment, but their resources are stretched too thin to help individual inmates. You can donate funds directly to support Amnesty's work for American women who are being mistreated in prison by logging on to www.amnesty.org, and the Legal Aid Society at www.legal-aid.org. (The Legal Aid Society recently laid off over a dozen people because of lack of funds.)

Don't get me wrong. If you break the law, you need to be punished. But let's be clear about this. Punished, not tortured and raped.

I hope my story helps educate the public on prison conditions for women.

I have had a unique personal experience with all these issues, and I believe I have an insight into them that can be very helpful to others.

Now that I am, in effect, going public, and I am telling my story, I am organizing a series of small discussion groups with teenage girls (and sometimes their mothers) where I talk about my experiences and offer suggestions on how to stay out of the type of trouble I got involved with as a teen. After my talk, the girls can ask me any questions they want.

Also a portion of the proceeds from this book and other business endeavors of mine will be donated to several organizations, including the Million Mom March, Amnesty International American prison projects, Legal Aid Society Prisoners' Rights Project, and various domestic violence organizations and shelters. Check my website, www.amyfisher.com, for updated information.

Chapter Thirty-Two

TURNING THIRTY

I am now thirty years old. I am a mother and wife. I am a journalist and an artist. I have spent the last twelve years turning my life around, piecing it back together. I am happy to be at this stage. It's a time of wisdom, something I was sorely lacking as a child. Thirty is a new beginning for me.

I try to live my life as a good, caring person. That's my biggest commitment to myself—that I'm good to all the people around me.

I would not be the person I am now at thirty without having gone through what I did. I probably would not have been as caring in the long run. I am more in tune with people's feelings now because I've put people through so much pain and I've been through so much pain.

As someone who once tried to kill herself, it saddens me when I hear about people who commit suicide and their family and friends say, "Why didn't they come to me? I loved them. I would have been there for them." Through that experience I make sure that I am there for the people around me.

I am a happy person now at thirty.

I could have definitely lived without my youthful experiences. Prison was a horrible experience, but it was also a reflective time. Any maturation and rehabilitation that I achieved, however, was through my own self-growth, not from being locked up and treated like crap.

Forgiveness is a wonderful trait. I think that when we forgive people for some wrong, it makes us better as people. I think forgiveness is nice if you can bring yourself to honestly feel it. Mary Jo has said she forgives me, and she helped me get out of prison early. I admire that strength. I wish I were that strong.

There are plenty of people who have done bad things to me in my life, and I forgive them. We move on. I don't care anymore. I don't think about it. I cannot forgive Joey, however, because he took me when I was so young and fragile, and he ruined my life. If it weren't for him, I would have gone on doing wacky, stupid teenage things. Eventually and more naturally I would have gotten to this mature point in my life. I would have grown up like everybody does. I would have gone on to college and some professional career. I wouldn't have harmed his wife and through that act hurt her children. I wouldn't have been in prison. I wouldn't have been the Long Island Lolita. And I blame him for that. He's a sexual predator, and he never paid for it. To this day he hasn't fully admitted it.

I could probably forgive him if he would say, "I apologize to Amy Fisher. I'm sorry, I know I have a problem, I'm seeking help for my problem." But for somebody to be so awful, so vicious, so coldhearted, to not accept that he did anything wrong and go on living his life in such a horrible, criminal manner, how could I forgive him?

I get a lot of mail from people who feel that I too was a victim in this whole story. I get mail from people who feel that I was not a victim but have since turned my life around and been rehabilitated and redeemed. There are also people who think I should be punished eternally for what I did as a child twelve years ago.

If I wasn't meant to go on with my life, I guess I should have been given the death penalty. What do those people want of me? To sit in a bare apartment, to not have a job, not get married, not have children, to go on welfare and have society support me? Do they think I should not tell my story—one that just might help someone else? Should I not use this unsolicited notoriety that has gone on for years beyond my fifteen minutes of fame to help other people?

We know at a certain age that we're going to have to get a job, that we're going to function in society, that we're going to have to be productive members of that society, so I'm doing what society tells me I'm supposed to do as a human being. I am fulfilling my role as a little gear in the system. Why shouldn't I try to better myself and take my terrible experience and use that in some way to make the world better? As I've said before, if one troubled girl learns from my experience, then I've accomplished something. And I'll tell you, there are hundreds of thousands of troubled girls, abused kids, and mixed-up adults out there who are headed for the same type of trouble I was involved with.

While most people don't commit violent crimes as teenagers, many teenagers at some point have premarital sex, get drunk, stay out late without their parents' knowledge, host wild parties when their parents go on vacation, or do something others might not approve of. As an adult, when you think back ten, fifteen, twenty years and remember your youthful indiscretions, you say, "How stupid was I to do any of those things?" As an adult, you know things like drinking and then driving your friends home is insane and reckless. You wouldn't do it now, but twenty years ago, when you were young and having fun, you didn't think about ramifications. It may not have been completely criminal, and you may not have been arrested, but it was still wrong and it was still juvenile. Truly my own behavior was criminal, but it was still juvenile. An adult with all her senses intact would have been too smart to do what I did.

I grew up. I matured. I have been productive. And I am happy that I have not let down my family, friends, and the countless people who have written to me over the years with their support. I hope I have made you proud.

When I was being resentenced on April 22, 1999, Judge Ira Wexner said to me, "You are still a young woman and could be a productive member of society if you channel your efforts in the proper manner. Based on the information I have received while you have been incarcerated, I believe you can do that."

Mary Jo Buttafuoco said to me: "I know how precious life is because I almost lost it...I have been given a second chance at life. You are being given a second chance too. I pray that you will take it and make something out of this awful tragedy...I pray for you and your continued recovery. Good luck."

I hope that Judge Wexner and Mary Jo are also pleased with the outcome.

EPILOGUE

On May 4, 2004, the *Long Island Press* was notified that Amy Fisher had won a Press Club Media Award for the prestigious and very competitive category "Column/News." The award is voted on by chapters of the highly regarded Society of Professional Journalists.

WARNING SIGNS

A ll parents want to believe their child is perfect. Well, at the very least, a good kid. It is this desperate need to believe in their child that causes parental blindness to emerge. If they're told their child stole something, they say, "Not my kid." If their child is caught red-handed, the parents say, "Well, I raised my child to have values. He won't do it again, he's truly remorseful." My parents definitely fell into this category.

When I was young, I was an easy kid. I always followed the rules and did what I was told. I didn't know I could rebel. It wasn't until I was a teenager and entered high school, where I was surrounded by teens older than myself, that I wanted to deviate from the cookie-cutter routine my parents had carefully laid out for me. My grades went from A's and B's to C's, D's, and F's—almost overnight. I didn't want to study. I wanted to have a good time. Why did I need school anyway? I was smart and I thought I already had all the answers.

My parents were rarely home, so when the unfavorable progress reports arrived in the mailbox, I'd throw them out. When the school left messages that I was absent or doing poorly, I erased the messages. When my report card arrived, I'd give it to my mother on a Monday so my parents would be over my failures by the following weekend and I'd be able to go out. They would yell, and I would say that I was trying but that school was just too hard. Perhaps if I had showed up a little more and actually read a textbook, the material wouldn't have been so perplexing.

Looking back, I think I didn't care because I felt my parents didn't care. Now, logically, I believe they did, but they left the problem for others to correct. Unfortunately, children aren't like a messy home—you can't just hire a maid. Screaming at me to do better was worthless. Paying for tutoring classes for me was laughable. Tutoring is for kids who want to better themselves but don't understand specific subject matter. I was a goof-off who needed positive structure and a massive amount of attention, which was painfully absent.

Unfortunately, once a teen's grades drop so dramatically, it's hard to recover on his or her own. It's a turning point where a parent has to be on top of the child's every move. The trust factor is over. Telling your child to do better and relying on him or her to do so alone is like putting a steak in front of a dog and expecting him not to eat it.

My father would scream at me and berate me for several days over my horrible report cards, and then all would be soon forgotten. He never asked how I was doing, if I did my homework, or if I found anything I was studying in the least bit interesting. For him, it was just another excuse to scream.

On the other hand, my mother cared but worked long hours; when she finally came home, she was tired. She provided a good life for me, and I attended great schools. She believed that the teachers would show me the way. I was a good kid. I was smart. I would be fine.

The failing grades, the numerous absences noted on the report cards, and the comments about poor progress in the remarks column were red flags missed by parents who were in denial.

By the time I was fourteen, I had a steady boyfriend. By the time I was fifteen, we were having sex. His parents traveled extensively, leaving him unattended. Most weekends I would sleep at his house. I would tell my parents I was sleeping at a girlfriend's home. They never once called to make sure I was there or to see if I was all right. I came and went as I pleased—not a word was ever said. My parents, again, trusted me. Why, I'll never know. It's not like I gave them a reason to.

By the time I was sixteen, all my friends and classmates were getting cars—a Mercedes for this one, a Corvette for that one. I assumed it was my right to have a car simply because the other spoiled brats had one. I had to fit in, didn't I? I whined and cried and, of course, begged. My parents saw the other kids with nice cars and figured if the other parents were doing it, well, maybe it wasn't so bad. They followed the other parents' lead and so began my crash course in destruction.

These are the biggest warning signs for a teen in trouble (from someone who learned the hard way):

- Problems with school grades and school attendance
- Lack of or a change in friends or clique
- A dramatic change in appearance
- Becoming nasty and argumentative
- Lack of participation in any school activities or sports
- Laziness; refusing to clean up after themselves
- Being idle (kids need to be active, to be involved in sports or working a part-time job)
- Sleeping all day
- Staying out late at night

Here are some ways to combat the problems. These suggestions would have changed the direction of my life:

1. Stay in touch weekly (or daily, if necessary) with teachers.

2. Make sure teachers have a direct contact number for you.

3. Have teachers give you a schedule of homework and tests on a weekly basis so that you can make sure your child does his or her work. That old "I did it in school" or "I have no homework" routine should no longer work on you.

4. Go over your child's assignments on a daily basis. Don't forget to praise achievement or extra effort.

5. If your teen is nasty, abusive, or refusing to get with the program, remind him or her that things like phones, the computer, the TV, and going out with friends are not givens in life: they should be regarded as privileges that can be taken away—and not just for a day or a week but until the child's behavior and productivity improve.

6. Be consistent with punishments.

7. To get your teen involved in activities, you may have to get involved also. Find out what the school offers and make your kid get off his or her butt and participate. A little sweat and hard work never hurt anyone. If your child refuses, then refuse them their privileges.

8. Getting to know your kid's friends as well as their parents is important. You should know where your child is at all times. If he or she says they are going out with Jane, well, call Jane's mother to say hello. Find out what their plans are. If they are going to John's house, get a phone number and address. A drive-by visit wouldn't hurt every once in a while.

9. If your teen is a diligent student who is busy after school with activities, then a part-time job is too much. A part-time job is more about learning responsibility than about earning money. A kid who does well is already learning responsibility. For a slacker, a job may be just what the doctor ordered. You'll know where your kid is, for starters. A job will also make your kid get up and do something productive. It might even show your know-it-all darling how hard he or she will have to work for minimum wage without a good education.

10. Oversleeping is an obvious sign of laziness and depression. No one should sleep his or her life away, so wake your teen up on the weekends. If your kid is not working and doesn't have plans with friends, perhaps you should spend time with him or her. Do not give your kid an option, in which case he or she can say, "No thanks," and continue lying around in pajamas and doing nothing. Make your kid get up, get dressed, and practice a little family bonding.

11. There is nothing positive to do at 2:00 A.M. that can't be done at 9:00 P.M. The clubs and bars don't start swinging till after 11:00 P.M., but hey, a teen has no business there anyway. Don't rest comfortably knowing it's illegal to let minors into these places — they still get in. And teens who can't get inside like to hang out in the bars' parking lots. It's doubtful that they are studying at a friend's house till 3:00 A.M.

12. Routines are good. Have your teen call in at the same designated time whenever he or she is out — just to check in. No matter where your kid is, or even if you know he or she is expected later. Besides keeping tabs on your teen, this is a way of pulling him or her out of a bad situation when necessary.

13. Set a curfew. If it's not followed, declare war. No privileges, nothing. Don't bend — you're the boss.

14. We all want to trust our kids. It is better, however, to be safe than sorry. Once in a while invade your teen's privacy. Poke around his or her room a little bit. You can learn a lot by reading a note written by a friend. You might find drugs, condoms, failing test papers. The possibilities are endless. (You may also find some wonderful, positive things instead!) This

kind of interference is for the greater good. Our children's futures are at stake. They might be angry now, but they will thank us someday when their lives are good thanks to our meddling.

15. Talk to your child. Be there for your child.

16. Be honest with your child. Answer his or her questions truthfully. Ask about friends, about school, about how his or her day went. You can ascertain a lot of information from a few simple questions. Let your teen know you can learn some interesting things from him or her.

Get your child help if you see trouble. It could make all the difference.

Gun Control Organizations

Alliance for Justice, Co/Motion

> (www.comotionmakers.org): Fosters youth leadership in social change. The site includes information on the Youth Gun Violence Prevention Initiative, which engages young people on the issue of gun violence.

American Bar Association, Special Committee on Gun Violence

> (www.abanet.org/gunviol): The website provides the ABA's policy on gun violence, a background report, congressional correspondence, and facts on gun violence in schools.

American Jewish Congress, petition to Congress
(www.ajcongress.org/ptchoice.htm): Send a petition through the American Jewish Congress calling for the passage of meaningful gun-control legislation: gun licensing, registration, and installation of safety devices on guns.

American Medical Association, Diagnostic and Treatment Guidelines on Violence and Abuse
(www.ama-assn.org/ama/pub/category/3548.html): Reviews the epidemiology of firearm injuries and deaths and describes types of firearms and ammunition and their different impacts on safety. The physician guidelines can be viewed online.

Americans for Gun Safety
(www.americansforgunsafety.com): A group that discusses the enforcement of existing gun laws, endorses legislation, and floats various firearm regulations, such as registration and licensing, litigation against firearms manufacturers, and other regulatory measures, briefly mentioning their pros and cons.

Brady Campaign to Prevent Gun Violence
(www.bradycampaign.org): This is the biggie. News, statistics, research, refutations of anti-control studies, resources, and links promoting pro-control policies. Addresses gun-rights issues. Also home to the Million Mom March.

Coalition to Stop Gun Violence, Educational Fund to Stop Gun Violence
(www.csgv.org): Composed of 44 civic, professional, and religious organizations and 100,000 individual members who advocate for a ban on the sale and

possession of handguns and assault weapons. The website includes an action guide, legislative information, and action alerts.

Common Sense About Kids and Guns
(www.kidsandguns.org): Provides home firearm storage and safety tips to protect children and teens from gun violence and gun accidents.

Doctors Against Handgun Injury
(www.doctorsagainsthandguninjury.org): A division of the New York Academy of Medicine representing over 600,000 doctors who believe they have a responsibility to lecture on gun safety because of the death and injury toll caused by shooting incidents.

Get Unloaded, Gun Safety and Education Campaign
(www.getunloaded.org): A site that features merchandise, concert announcements, and safety tips.

Goodbyeguns.org
(www.goodbyeguns.org/index.html): An online petition to ban all guns in the United States.

Handgun Epidemic Lowering Plan (HELP) Network
(www.helpnetwork.org): An international network of medical and allied organizations and individuals dedicated to furthering gun control in the United States.

Handgun-Free America
(www.handgunfree.org): Research, quotes, commentary, and links supporting the banning of civilian handgun ownership.

Join Together

(www.jointogether.org): A clearinghouse for information on anti-gun violence.

Legal Community Against Violence

(www.lcav.org): An organization dedicated to reducing gun violence through legislation, litigation, and education. Provides financial and pro bono legal support for litigation and assistance to local governments defending ordinance challenges from gun-rights advocates.

Mothers Against Guns

(www.mothersagainstguns.org): Committed to ending gun violence in our communities and our nation by continuing to raise public awareness of the effect that gun violence has on our lives.

Mothers Against Teen Violence

(www.matvinc.org): The website provides a mission statement, information on counseling services and starting a chapter, and member-only services.

New Yorkers Against Gun Violence

(www.nyagv.org): Membership information, news, and pro–gun control links are available at the site.

PAX: Real Solutions to Gun Violence

(www.paxusa.org): The site provides news, facts, links, and information on how to get involved.

Stop Gun Violence

(www.stopgunviolence.org): Clearinghouse for information about gun-control organizations.

Source Notes

I used the following supporting documents, which are part of the public record, to recall, confirm, and supply facts for the book— especially, but not exclusively, the chapters and sections dealing with the legal aspects of my case, my relationships with Joey Buttafuoco and Eric Naiburg, and my description of and charges against Albion Correctional Facility and its guards. I also used articles from *The New York Times*, *Newsday*, *The New York Times Magazine*, the *Rochester Democrat and Chronicle*, the *New York Post*, the *Buffalo News*, the *Daily News*, *Time* magazine, the Associated Press, the *Los Angeles Times*, *New York* magazine, Gannett News Service, *People* magazine, and transcripts of news reports and interviews aired on ABC news programs, CBS-Radio, 1010-WINS Radio, CNN, Court TV, WB11, E!, NBC news programs, *The Howard Stern Show*, *Geraldo*, *Dateline*, *Inside Edition*, *Headliners and Legends*, *The Today Show*, *The Phil Donahue Show*, *Burden of Proof*, *E! True Hollywood Story*, *American Justice*, and *Hard Copy*. I want to thank Gary Craig of the *Rochester Democrat and Chronicle* and Lisa Freeman and Dori Lewis of the Legal Aid Society Prisoners' Rights Project for supplying further information, research, and documentation.

——Nassau County Police Department, Amy Fisher, written statement, May 22, 1992, 2:35 A.M.

——County Court, Nassau County, Transcript, Amy Fisher, Plea, June 2, 1992.

——County Court, Nassau County, Transcript, Bail Reduction Hearing, June 6, 1992.

——County Court, Nassau County, Transcript, Peter Guagenti, Arraignment, June 12, 1992.

——Nassau County District Attorney Denis Dillon and Assistant District Attorney Fred Klein, document to Eric Naiburg: oral statements made to police upon Amy Fisher's arrest, June 16, 1992.

——Supreme Court of the State of New York, County of Nassau, Change of Plea, September 23, 1992.

——*Hard Copy* transcript, September 24, 1992.

——Eric Naiburg to Honorable Marvin Goodman, Nassau County Court, Pre-Sentence Memorandum, November 9, 1992.

——County Court, Nassau County, Transcript, Amy Fisher, Sentencing, December 1, 1992.

——County Court, Nassau County, Transcript, Peter Guagenti, Sentencing, February 4, 1993.

——Supreme Court of the State of New York, County of Nassau, Stipulation of Settlement: Mary Jo Buttafuoco, Amy Fisher, Roseann Fisher, Elliot Fisher, Peter Guagenti, Joseph Buttafuoco, Vanguard Insurance Company, Hartford Underwriters Insurance, June 29, 1993.

——Kathryn Cunningham, Esq., letter to Dominic Barbara, Esq., regarding Amy Fisher's Victim's Satement at Time of Sentencing of Joey Buttafuoco, October 19, 1993.

——Phone transcript between Rose Fisher and Albion guard Sgt. Schwartz, October 22, 1993.

——County Court, Nassau County, letter to Dominic Barbara, Esq., regarding Joseph Buttafuoco, Indictment 84604, Victim's Statement at Time of Sentencing, November 1993.

——Albion Correctional Facility, transcript of Disciplinary Tier Hearing for "shoe" infraction, March 12, 1997.

——Denis Dillon, District Attorney, letter to Pedro L. Hernandez, New York State Division of Parole, notification of Amy Fisher's cooperation in investigation against Joey Buttafuoco, April 1, 1997.

——Philip Catapano, letter to Brian D. Travis, Chairman, Board of Parole, parole application of Amy Fisher, April 9, 1997.

——Office of the District Attorney, County of Nassau, Nassau County District Attorney Denis Dillon, letter to William Callahan, New York State Division of Parole, April 27, 1999, regarding "legal representation that she [Amy Fisher] received [from Eric Naiburg] was constitutionally deficient."

―― Terrence X. Tracy, letter to Philip Catapano, Esq., regarding Parole Board interview with Amy Fisher, May 6, 1997.

―― County Court, County of Nassau, Eric Naiburg statement regarding "promises" by the District Attorney's office regarding parole, May 23,1997

―― Patricia Weiss, Esq., letter to Terrence X. Tracy, Division of Parole, Albany, New York, regarding Amy Fisher Parole Board matter: Mary Jo Buttafuoco's waiver of rights, May 27, 1997.

―― State of New York, Executive Department, Division of Parole, Minutes of Parole Board Hearing, Initial Appearance, June 10, 1997.

―― State of New York, Executive Department, Division of Parole, Inmate Status Report for parole board appearance, June 2, 1997.

―― Parole interview, June 2,1997.

―― U.S. District Court, Western District of New York, Buffalo, *New York, Roseann Fisher and Amy Fisher, Plaintiffs, v. Glenn S. Goord, et al., Defendants* (suit against Albion Correctional Facility and guards), decision and order, filed July 16, 1997.

―― U.S. District Court, Amended Complaint, Glenn S. Goord, Acting Commissioner of the State of New York, State Department of Correctional Services, et al., August 15, 1997.

―― Board of Parole, Appeals Unit, *Amy Fisher v. New York State Board of Parole*, Administrative Parole Appeal, September 18, 1997.

―― State of New York, Executive Department, Division of Parole, Statement of Appeals Unit Findings, February 2, 1998.

―― County Court, County of Nassau, Affidavit by Amy Fisher, April 5, 1998.

―― County Court, County of Nassau, Reply Affirmation, April 27,1998.

Exhibits:

Exhibit "C": Matchbook with note from Eric Naiburg, to Amy Fisher, November 3, 1992.

Exhibit "D", Amy Fisher Affidavit, September 14, 1998.

Exhibit "E" Eric Naiburg, to Amy Fisher, handwritten poem and drawing of outline of hand, December 9, 1992.

Exhibit "F": Eric Naiburg, to Amy Fisher, handwritten poem, December 12, 1992.

Exhibit "H": Eric Naiburg, to Amy Fisher, handwritten note and drawings, February 19, 1993.

Exhibits G, I-Z, A1-C1: Eric Naiburg, letters to Amy Fisher, December 9, 12, and 22, 1992; January 5, 7, 9, and 25, 1993; February 4, 18, 19, 22, and 25, 1993; March 11 and 22, 1993; April 2, 1993; May 6, 19, and 24, 1993; August 4, 1993; November 2, 1993; May 2 and 27, 1994; April 10, 1995; February 13, 1998.

——— County Court, County of Nassau, Notice of Motion, April 28, 1998.

——— County Court, County of Nassau, Memorandum of Law, April 28, 1998.

——— County Court, County of Nassau, Supplemental Memorandum of Law, May 25, 1998.

——— County Court, County of Nassau, Nassau County Police Detective, Martin Alger, Affidavit, regarding Fred Klein and Eric Naiburg, June 5,1998.

——— County Court, County of Nassau, Nassau County District Attorney Denis Dillon, Affirmation, regarding Eric Naiburg, June 8,1998.

——— Supreme Court of the State of New York, County of Albany, *Amy Fisher v. Brion Travis, Chairman, New York State Board of Parole*, Verified Petition For a Judgment Pursuant to Article 78 of the Civil Practice Law and Rules, June 15, 1998.

——— Supreme Court of the State of New York, County of Albany, *Amy Fisher v. Brion Travis, Chairman, New York State Board of Parole*, Affidavit In Support Of Order To Show Cause, For a Judgment Pursuant to Article 78 of the Civil Practice Law and Rules, June 15, 1998.

——— Supreme Court of the State of New York, County of Albany, *Amy Fisher v. Brion Travis, Chairman, New York State Board of Parole*, Affidavit In Support Of Motion To Proceed As A Poor Person, For a Judgment Pursuant to Article 78 of the Civil Practice Law and Rules, June 15, 1998.

——— County Court, County of Nassau, Affirmation in Opposition to Defendant's Motion to Vacate a Judgment of Conviction, June 18, 1998.

——— County Court, County of Nassau, Assistant District Attorney Fred Klein, Affirmation, June 18, 1998.

——— State of New York, Supreme Court, County of Albany, *Amy Fisher v. Brion Travis, Chairman, New York State Board of Parole*, Order to Show Cause, For a Judgment Pursuant to Article 78 of the Civil Practice Law and Rules, July 8, 1998.

——— Affidavit of Service, State of New York, County of Orleans, July 23, 1998.

——— Supreme Court of the State of New York, County of Albany, *Amy Fisher v. Brion Travis, Chairman, New York State Board of Parole*, Notice of Motion To Dismiss The Petition, For a Judgment Pursuant to Article 78 of the Civil Practice Law and Rules, August 17, 1998.

——— Supreme Court of the State of New York, County of Albany, *Amy Fisher v. Brion Travis, Chairman, New York State Board of Parole*, Affirmation, For a Judgment Pursuant to Article 78 of the Civil Practice Law and Rules, August 17, 1998

—— Bruce Barket, P.C., letter to Eric Naiburg, regarding request response to affidavits filed by District Attorney's office requesting forwarding "all correspondence from Amy Fisher over the past six years," August 28, 1998.

—— Bruce Barket, P.C., letter to Eric Naiburg, regarding plan to file motion in Nassau County Court alleging improper personal and sexual relationship with client Amy Fisher, August 28, 1998.

—— Eric Naiburg, letter to Bruce Barket, P.C., regarding Amy Fisher, August 31, 1998, responding to Bruce Barket, P.C., letter of August 28, 1998.

—— Raymond G. Perini, attorney for Eric Naiburg, letter to Honorable Ira H. Wexner, Nassua County Court, September 22, 1998.

—— County Court, County of Nassau, Reply Affirmation, December 7, 1998.

—— Affirmation of Eric Naiburg, February 2, 1999.

—— County Court, County of Nassau, Affirmation in response to order to show cause, March 8, 1999.

—— County Court, Nassau County, Affirmation in Response to Defendant's Motion to Vacate Judgment, March 30, 1999.

—— Mary Jo Buttafuoco, letter to Denis Dillon, Nassau County District Attorney, regarding early release for Amy Fisher, March 1999.

—— Bruce Barket, P.C., letter to William Callahan, Facility Parole Officer, Division of Parole, Albion State Prison, regarding matter of Amy Fisher, April 2, 1999.

—— Aristedes Soto, Albion Correction Facility, letter to Judge Ira H. Wexner, April 21, 1999.

—— Guidance Information Management System, Albion Correctional Facility, Assessment of Inmate, Program Assignments, Disciplinary Incident Summary, April 21, 1999.

—— County Court, Nassau County, Plea and Sentence, April 22, 1999.

—— Supreme Court of the State of New York, County of Nassau, Honorable Ira H. Wexner, Supreme Court Justice, Decision on Motion, April 22, 1999.

—— Lisa Ullman, Assistant Attorney General, letter to State of New York, Office of the Attorney General, Honorable Bernard J. Malone, Justice of the Supreme Court, regarding matter of *Fisher v. Board of Parole*, May 3, 1999.

—— Robert H. Straus, Chief Counsel, State of New York Grievance Committee for the Second and Eleventh Judicial Districts, letter regarding Eric Naiburg, Esq., June 1, 1999.

About the Authors

In 1992 **Amy Fisher** was thrust into the limelight as the sixteen-year-old girl suddenly known around the world as the "Long Island Lolita" after she shot her thirty-six-year-old boyfriend's wife. She has been the subject of three movies and several books, but now, at thirty years old, she is telling her own story for the first time in *If I Knew Then….* In an inspirational account of rehabilitation and redemption, Amy's life has made a dramatic turnaround. She has become an award-winning columnist for the *Long Island Press*, an artist-entrepreneur, a devoted wife and mother, and an advocate for several social causes. She and co-author Robbie Woliver are currently working on a new non-fiction true-crime book.

Robbie Woliver, co-author of *If I Knew Then…* is the editor-in-chief of the *Long Island Press*, and has edited Amy Fisher's column since it began in June 2002. An award-winning journalist and editor, he has been a columnist for *Newsday*, senior editor at the *Long Island Voice*, and a writer for the *The New York Times*. He has also written for many other publications and media outlets, including the *Village Voice*, *Rolling Stone*, *CBS Market Watch*, *Salon*, *BankRate*, and the *San Francisco Chronicle*. He is the founder of the National Music Awards, owner of the legendary music venue Folk City, and author of *Wyoming & March*, *Bringing It All Back Home*, *Hoot!* and a new novel, *Creation*.